THE ADVENTURES OF

BUG
& ME

THE ADVENTURES OF

BUG & ME

NONA FREEMAN

The Adventures of Bug & Me

by Nona Freeman

©1977 Word Aflame Press
Hazelwood, MO 63042-2299
Printing History: 1977, 1980, 1983, 1987, 2010

ISBN 0-912315-28-8

Cover Design by Tim Cummings

All Scripture quotations in this book are from the KIng James Version of the Bible unless otherwise identified.

Printed in United States of America

WORD AFLAME PRESS
8855 Dunn Road, Hazelwood, MO 63042
www.pentecostalpublishing.com

To Bug
My Inspiration and My Anchor

Thanks

I am deeply indebted to the many wonderful people who inspired, encouraged, insisted, and assisted, according to the need.

Thetus Tenney stimulated a lazy mind.

Norma Davis typed and said, "Hurry!"

David Wheeler prodded.

The late Arthur Clanton reminded.

Carolyn Hudson deciphered and retyped.

God bless all!

Contents

Foreword

The fascinating world of foreign missions has been created by fascinating people! *The Adventures of Bug & Me* gives the reader the feeling he's peeking . . . catching an inside view of what makes a missionary family tick. For those of us who know the Freemans, this comes as no surprise, for they are not pretentious people. They have always lived their lives and commitment to the cause of the Lord Jesus Christ with candor.

It appears that from the time Nona Bertha Eastridge made her grand entrance into the world at Shuler, Arkansas, in 1916, she has kept it hopping. Her taking hold of the meaning of life early was characterized by her water baptism in the name of Jesus Christ in 1925. Two years later, she was filled with the baptism of the Holy Spirit in Durham, Oklahoma.

It was no accident, as we are all witnesses, that Nona married Elpho Letris (known affectionately as "Bug") Freeman in the year 1937. They soon started preaching together (1939), and in May of that year acknowledged their call to Africa. No time was wasted in seeking an audience with the Foreign Missions Board, which met that fall in East St. Louis, Illinois.

Their early ministry took them from pastoring in Portales, New Mexico, to evangelizing throughout the Rio Grande Valley in Texas. The year 1941 found them accepting the pastorate of a little church in Rosepine, Louisiana, where they remained until leaving for South Africa in 1948 to fulfill their missionary appointment. The E. L. Freemans were blessed with five children: Sandra '38, Dale '40, Lynda '42, Sharon '45, and Marla '47. Many happy moments, as well as the near tragic, are related in these pages. It's been often said, and it must be true: "There just isn't anything like doing missionary work!" It seems I can almost hear five faint "amens."

At the time of this writing, the Freemans have devoted twenty-nine years to missionary work in Africa. This time includes the several furloughs spent back in the States. The first furlough came for Brother Freeman in 1953. Sister Freeman took her first one the following year after her husband's return. Joint furloughs followed in 1958, 1965, and 1971.

During these strenuous years, the Freemans were able to witness a strong work established in South Africa. Their efforts in loving the lost, along with the contributions made by additional missionaries over the years, account for a present total of approximately 130 national workers and over 11,500 believers.

During their 1971 furlough, an appointment was made which broadened the Freeman's ministry to include the entire continent of Africa as he was selected as Regional Field Supervisor for that area. Although this assignment takes them into many countries on the African continent and brings them back to the States for annual board meetings and a promotional tour, they continue to make their home in South Africa.

Nona has been a good soldier and has mastered the art of living out of a suitcase. Her easy flow to living is perhaps best detected as she eases into your family room wearing her robe and slippers, gets comfortable, and with gusto attacks the hook and yarn. When she isn't crocheting, she's sewing. When she isn't doing either, she's preaching. Her unique talent for perceiving the needs of the people to whom she is ministering aligns itself very closely with that of an old family doctor. . . . No time is lost. It hurts for just a moment, but you feel better right away.

If you ever thought for one moment that missionaries were made of perfection and cast in bronze, then read the book. You'll soon see they're made of steel and cast to the four corners of a dying world!

Introduction

"Write!" many esteemed friends urged.
"You should share your experiences."
"Write! It would prove such a blessing."
"You are robbing us!" one said dogmatically.

Study and note-making efforts had been in operation for some time, each one appearing more helpless than the previous one. How to begin? I could not find the answer.

Our Lord, however, works in wondrous ways—a particularly virulent virus attacked a weary body and flattened it! When I was able to think at all, I began to praise the Lord. I thanked Him for the flu and all its uncomfortable aspects. I especially thanked Him that the limit of strength was reached in our little travel trailer.

When I felt like opening my eyes, I looked out on a tranquil, green valley and the imperturbable mountains on the other side. My window was a picture framed by silver oak and blue eucalyptus leaves gently swaying in the breeze. In a climate of worship, the most Beloved of all friends graced every waking hour with His presence, real and sweet. And one day, shortly thereafter, instruction and inspiration came hand in hand.

"Start with your furlough story. Write in the mood of the gracious South African custom of friends' meeting across the dainty tea service and being mellowed by the fragrant brew into nostalgic confidences."

Shirking from the obviously necessary "me phrases," I must assert, if there is any merit or some good is achieved, it has been in spite of "me." All honor and credit must go to Jesus, the all-wise Potter, Who specializes in remaking broken, worthless vessels.

Many names and places are deliberately vague to avoid monotony and offense. I have a deep, sincere love and appreciation for the entire unique and precious family of God's children. I share my heart with you.

I am deeply grateful to all the wonderful people who have helped me with this little, yet not so little, endeavor. The practical assistance, loving encouragement, and inspiration will never be forgotten.

Gratitude to my dear Lord includes a wonder of the long-suffering that endured my density and slowness to understand what it was all about:

"Learn to trust Me, child."

Chapter One

Bug and I Get Started

It all started when the Freeman family teetered up the rope gangplank of the *SS Genevieve Lykes* on that blustery March day in 1948. New Orleans had been lashed by such violent storms the past few days that a ship had run aground in the mouth of the Mississippi. Cars and homes were being lapped by the dirty flood-waters, and it became necessary to deliver groceries by rowboat.

Two additional adults and five extra children had strained the seams of the home of our genial host, Johnny Thomas. There had been six days of forced confinement until the waters had receded and the seven Freemans were able to move to the roomier quarters of the cargo boat bound for Cape Town, South Africa.

Sandra (nine) and Dale (seven) demonstrated their agility by making numerous trips up and down the wobbly gangplank. Lynda (five), Sharon (two), and Marla (six months) acquiesced to being carried on once. There had been an epidemic of coughing flu

17

that winter, but the five Freeman children had escaped it—or so we thought. Three days out to sea, Lynda, Sharon, and Maria began to whoop with strangling coughing attacks. How we "whooped it up" across the Atlantic is another story, but somehow we made it in spite of the captain's strongly expressed displeasure.

We knew that after four to seven years in Africa a furlough would be due, but in those early years such weighty matters as adjustment, language complications, and pioneering with the whole gospel took priority.

By July 1952 we must have had some vague thoughts about furlough but not many. We were in Durban, 400 miles from home, for special services. Some friends, who were away, loaned us their home and cook.

Everyone was asleep that night by the time I had straightened books, picked up sandals and hair ribbons, and gratefully stretched out on my side of the bed. Then the strangest thing happened. I distinctly heard the words: "A preview of future events."

Pictures (as slides) began to flash in front of me. They were of us! We were frantically trying to complete a red brick building. (I thought it was a church, for we were wrestling with red tape to get ground for one in Durban on that trip.) I saw tent services in progress. I saw myself helping my big Irishman pack. I watched myself tell him good-bye at the airport. Part of my mind was aware of shock when he said he would be gone six months.

Bug and I Get Started

The disturbingly clear pictures kept flashing. I was working alone, preaching alone, sitting by the bedside of a sick child alone. There were other scenes I did not understand, some intimating danger. Then I saw the head of the house being welcomed home again, and the next few scenes showed us traveling and preaching together.

"Now it is your turn to go; I'll help you pack." My anguished cry of "No!" was so real I woke up trembling. "No! No! I don't want to go alone."

Too troubled to sleep, I wakened my husband to tell him what I had seen.

"Now, look, Nona, if you think I am going anywhere and leave you and the children for several months because of a dream or a nightmare, you are badly mistaken. I think you ate too much curried cauliflower for supper last night!"

I fervently hoped so and tried to forget the whole affair, but two weeks later, when we returned home, a letter was there from the Missions Department, outlining a plan for separate furloughs. Soon after, some invisible providential wheels started turning toward providing us a home. The anxiety of the dream and letter was shoved into the background.

There is an intimate family fact that should be explained. There was this enterprising baby with confused gears. He crawled backwards! From the habit of looking over his shoulder and backing rapidly to his target, he was nicknamed "Bug." Because his real names were rather unusual, the pet name stuck. Later, I met and married Bug. What he is has given that humble name amazing qualities—unconscious dignity, gentle humor, humility, complete honesty, and total dedication. My worst fight against irritation is when someone hears the name for the first time and responds with a silly giggle, "Hi, Bugsy!"

Early in 1952, Bug sat up suddenly in bed one morning and declared emphatically, "The Lord is going to help me build us a house." I contributed the cold water. "You must have bumped your head! There is often no money for daily necessities. How can you build a house without a penny of capital?"

"I don't know," he affirmed, "but we need an adequate place to live, so Jesus is going to do it!" Though I forgot about the declaration, the unseen wheels were turning—on faith! First, an independent missionary gave us some tithes (the only time that ever happened). "Use this for a deposit on a building lot. Someday you can build your own home!"

Then, our building inspector neighbor (employee of the city) offered to draw us a house plan. "And I'll get it approved at the municipal offices when you're ready to build."

"It will be a long, long time before that happens!" I thought.

A German doctor of zoology, whom we befriended when he first came to South Africa, came to see us one day and said in his quaint accent, "I have come into some money and would like to help you folks. I will loan you $1,600. Pay it back when and as you can. Buy building materials, start your house, and when the money is gone, go to the Building Society and they will loan you money. You can pay off the lot and finish your house."

Bug and I Get Started

There were some technicalities—like persuading the seller to transfer the title deed of the ground to our name on the strength of a small deposit (one payment and a promise)! But all obstacles melted, and miraculously, construction began in November 1952.

We were doing as much of the work as possible. In December we moved into three small utility rooms in the first building erected on the back of the property. Then the letter came: "Brother Freeman, your furlough begins February 1953." He asked for a delay until April, which was granted. The intense activity, as seen in the "preview" around a red brick building, had begun! (For economical reasons, all construction in South Africa is masonry.)

We interspersed our work with tent meetings and revival services in Johannesburg. Overly abundant rainfall provided other interruptions. But, the *blessing side* of the ledger stacked high! Many neighborhood youngsters put in long hours helping. (Quite out of character. The Lord must have moved on them!) Our inspector friend said, "I'll put in the shelves and hang the doors." He had already nailed up the ceiling.

When D day arrived, only the kitchen was completed and in use. Outside doors were still needed, and only the ceilings had been painted. I was very apprehensive about the business end of this operation because I had never had such responsibility before. I followed Bug around asking questions, and unfortunately, in the confusion, all the answers did not register.

The very last night we dragged our mattress up to one of the bedrooms that had a door so Bug could

21

spend at least one night in the new home before he left. No one slept very much, however. Daffy, our cocker spaniel, was so alarmed about the children in one building and us in another that she spent the night racing up and down the stairs, barking alternately at our door and then theirs.

Chapter Two

Life
Without Bug

Several weeks of scraping, sanding, painting, and cleaning followed before we were able to move in. Our temporary abode was uncomfortable and crowded, but cozy. When our few sticks of furniture were finally scattered throughout the big house, there was more loneliness than jubilation. The first night I lay tense and jumpy, listening to every creak of the roof timbers and all the usual night noises that can be so ominous to an overactive imagination.

"That's someone at the kitchen window! Now they're trying to get in the back door." I trembled and thought to myself: "What a failure I am! Where is my God?" The miserable night ended with a prayer meeting and another lesson in TRUST.

Since Bug, the head of the house, describes most events as "not so good," "pretty good," or "good," there is still much not known about that first furlough. The first six weeks were spent in the Gold Coast (now Ghana), Nigeria, and Liberia. In a fact-finding tour of the Gold Coast and Nigeria, there were rough rides on native buses, trucks, and trains, not to mention uncertain accommodations.

There had been some correspondence with a would-be preacher in Nigeria. One letter requested a typewriter. A later one, a car. "He'll want an airplane next," was the dry comment from one of our African preachers.

But when Bug arrived at Abak, the man was in jail for theft. Disappointed, he walked up and down the narrow road with a heavy burden, the same burden he felt for every place he had visited. Sprawling dirty towns . . . Grassy plains . . . Remote jungle.

"Oh, God, let Thy name be declared here in Spirit and in Truth. Let Thy light shine in this darkness. Let men and women experience the new birth in Christ Jesus!"

There is a beautiful sequel to all the places where that heart cry went up. The answer today stands in buildings for worship, training centers, and great companies of the redeemed!

Bug felt impressed to leave Accra a week ahead of schedule for Roberts Field, Liberia. When the originally planned flight arrived a week later, it crashed on landing!

The tropical rain streamed steadily down on the jungle trail. The porter found the middle knob on the bottom of the suitcase hurt his head, so he turned it over and carried it upside down. The only problem was that the suitcase lid fit loosely over the bottom section, and all its contents were waterlogged by the time the mission station was reached.

Alone one night in a small, one room building, Bug fell asleep listening to the cheerful croak of frogs outside. Later, he was wakened by frogs in the room, and with them, an evil presence. They seemed to be chanting in unison: "Nye, nye, Pentecost! Nye, nye, Pentecost!" He sat up. "There seems to be three of us here, and there is only room for two. I plan to stay and Jesus will stay with me, so, Satan, you can leave at once!" There was instant stillness, and the rest of the night was peaceful.

A small plane took him the equivalent of a three and a half day's walk toward Fasama Mission, which was fortunate, for the day and a half that he did walk produced heel-to-toe blisters. On the return trip, he borrowed some tennis shoes which were more suitable for walking.

One of the missionary ladies suddenly remembered that someone had sent her a camera with a flash attachment. "Oh, Brother Freeman, I'll just go get my camera. This service would make such a good picture." The flash came in the middle of his sermon and ended the service rather abruptly. The whole congregation disappeared into the jungle!

Furlough was also due for veteran missionary Pauline Gruse. Arrangements were made for her to be an additional passenger in the small plane. The day and a half walk to the meeting place necessitated an overnight stop at a jungle village. There are always huts set aside in these places for travelers, but they were all full when they arrived.

"We have no place for you to stay," the chief firmly declared. Quite a palaver ensued. Bug silently reminded the Lord: "You said if I forsook houses, or brethren, or sisters, or father, or mother, or wife, or children, there would be a hundredfold more. All we need now is shelter for the night."

A headman, disturbed by the noise, came out of his hut to investigate. "Oh," he said, "I will make a place." He emptied huts by shoving out dogs, goats, drowsy children, and wives. New mats made by tying together the center rib of palm leaves alternating big ends with small ends were laid on crude beds. Although Bug's back felt slightly corrugated the next morning, the Lord did not fail to provide.

There were some anxious moments when the plane was late, and more anxiety when it finally came and the pilot compared the weight of his proposed load with the tiny runway. He backed the plane up into the bushes to give a few more feet for clearance, but there was a dangerous moment when, barely in the air, the tail dropped, almost touching the trees. One passenger had frozen, with closed eyes, on boarding. The other two prayed, and slowly altitude was gained.

They landed safely and gratefully on the Monrovian beach. The pilot avowed, "I'm not going back into the bush under those circumstances again. I'll kill myself and maybe someone else, too!" When the lady, known affectionately as "Mother Goose," heard what had happened, she grabbed the side of the plane as her knees buckled. Later, she was to become an intrepid air traveler, but that first experience was so terrifying that she canceled her trip home by plane and went by boat.

After a few more hazardous truck rides, jungle trails, and a monkey bridge river crossing, Bug left West Africa for America. That same week we received our first long awaited news from our traveler. All the letters posted at various times and places arrived the same day.

Daffy had been given a lecture on Bug's final day in South Africa: "You take good care of my wife while I'm gone." She became a dog with a mission. Before, she had been the children's pal, and her only interest in me had been as a benefactress with the food dish. Now, she shadowed my every move. If I painted late, she lay by the paint bucket and opened a reproachful eye every time the brush came by. If I sewed or wrote letters, she was under my chair. When I cooked, she was under my feet. Neighborhood children, accustomed to coming and going at will, were held at the gate for my approval.

The last week in June, a messenger of the Court delivered a summons to the door. Dismayed, I examined the document. It said, in effect, that E. L. Freeman (Bug) must pay $1,600 in three days, or all our movable property would be seized. This was the amount owed the doctor for the property we had purchased. To safeguard him, we had given a bond that stated specifically we would begin repayment in

January 1953. When matters were complicated by Bug's leaving, a verbal agreement had been reached to begin in July. I couldn't understand what was happening.

Daffy took one look at my troubled face and sunk her teeth into the man's ankle. I pulled her off, apologized, and refused to accept the summons. After all, it was issued to E. L. Freeman!

"If you have the power of attorney," he threatened, "I'll be back, and you will have to take it. And there better not be a dog in sight, or I'll make another case against you!"

Hurriedly, I tried to contact the doctor but learned that he was on an expedition to the Congo for spider research (spiders were his specialty). His wife was in Germany on holiday. His lawyer had discovered the bond and filed suit. Though not authorized by the doctor, the suit was legally correct. In an hour, the messenger was back, and I had to accept the summons. I started trying to trace Bug by phone, with no idea of his whereabouts. I did not know if he had reached America yet. My last letter was from Liberia.

I sat by the phone most of the next day. When, at last, that dear, familiar voice came through, I tried to keep the sound of tears out of my voice though they rained down my face.

"Don't worry," he comforted. "Just phone our lawyer, and ask him to handle the case on my instructions. He will advance whatever it takes to settle it. Go on to Durban for the special services as planned."

"Impossible. Dear, I've paid out everything on

28

building and paint accounts. I have passengers who will pay for the gas going down, but there is no food money. . . ."

"Pack a lunch," he answered succinctly, "and I'll send you money at Durban. This is Thursday. You should leave early Saturday morning. I'll be praying for you. Everything will be all right."

The lawyer was kind and understanding (after he knew there were definite instructions from Bug). Aunt Lil and Uncle Hans Botes, true friends, offered to let Sandra and Maria come to Durban with them a week later. This made room for the paying passengers in my car. I got off on schedule.

Traffic was heavy when we reached Durban just after 4:00 P.M. I was surprised but not apprehensive when a policeman pulled me over. "Madam, your car is illegal, and you will have to come with me."

"But, how, what—I don't understand," I gulped. Panic-stricken, I listened to his explanation.

"Your third party insurance disc should have been renewed and put on your windshield by May first, and here it is July!"

"I didn't know," I stammered. "I thought my husband took care of everything." This only infuriated the policeman.

"You cannot drive this car another foot!" he exploded.

"Sir," I pleaded, "I have small children, and I must take them to the friends we are visiting here." While he glared at me, my heart cried, "O Jesus, I need You *now*." There was nothing more I could say. I hoped I had a pleading look on my face. I waited, hardly daring to breathe.

Then gruffly, "All right. Take your children, but you are not to drive this car this weekend, and see that you are at 'C' Court on Monday morning at 9:00 A.M." He shook a threatening finger: "You are already in trouble, but if you fail to come to Court, it is going to be double trouble!" Thankfully, I assured him I would be there.

Three services later, on Sunday night, I was confronted with concrete evidence of another disaster for which I was not prepared. Serious internal trouble was brewing within our largest church. This was the proverbial straw that broke the camel's back. There was a sudden twisting pain in my chest as I collapsed onto the mattress on the floor where I had been sleeping during our stay in Durban. That night was the start of a four-year span of heart seizures, intervals of acute misery, before the healing touch came once and for all in 1957.

The most enormous problem this "camel" had was forgetting that Romans 8:28 is in the Book. It is the stabilizer, planned for the child of God by an all-wise Father. If one believes that "all things work together for good" and trusts Jesus to handle the "working," it is natural and precious to obey the many injunctions and to *rejoice* in thanksgiving for "all things," no matter the circumstances. How different this story would have been, "if only."

The whole miserable night the pendulum swung between pain and panic about "C" Court at 9:00 A.M. Too soon the court was reached, and the accused was called to stand in one of the loneliest spots ever.

Charges were read, and faltering explanations were given in a weak voice.

"Louder!" barked the magistrate. "I can't hear you."

The explanations were repeated with all the strength I could muster, which was still not enough for the frowning judge. My words were repeated inaccurately by nearby officials, and a sarcastic tirade assaulted me like a torrent.

"The public is warned continually by the radio and press of the deadline for Third Party Insurance. Would you have me to believe you neither heard nor read?" He didn't pause for an answer, and it would not have helped to tell the truth.

"No sir, we don't have a radio, and newspapers are a luxury we have done without for several months. Everything has gone toward our goal—a home."

The harsh voice went on and on. I felt myself swaying. "O Jesus, please don't let me faint."

He reached a climax and leaned forward as he thundered, "You are the eight hundredth motorist to enter our city without a valid Third Party. My patience is exhausted. I will make an example of you and all that follow you. I fine you fifteen pounds (42 dollars at that time) or thirty days in jail."

That suspended-in-space feeling again. I cautiously put my hand in my pocket and felt my total monetary assets. Nine pence (about eleven cents). The more I concentrated on standing straight, the more I swayed. It was at this point that I realized this was one of the questions I had asked Bug. The answer, however, had not registered. I had a flashback to an early morning scene. As Bug shaved, I asked from the bathroom door, "What about the insurance, dear?"

"It's all taken care of except . . ." That "except" had brought me here!

The friend who brought me to Court was waiting for a salary check. He said, "Your Honor, I have four pounds ($19.50). Would you accept this and give us until 4:00 P.M. to get the rest?"

"Absolutely not! Fifteen pounds now, or she goes straight to jail!" I clutched my nine pence and felt as devastated as if I were already there.

"Your Honor, I will pay that fine." Astonished, I turned to see that Uncle Hans had spoken. Aunt Lil was with him. They led me lovingly out of "C" Court.

"Oh, thank you, thank you! I could see myself in jail. How did you get here so soon? I didn't expect you until the end of the week. And how did you find me?" Patiently, they explained.

"We had the feeling you were in trouble, so we came on. We reached town early this morning and heard the news. After hunting this court for quite a while, we walked in the door just as the judge said: 'Fifteen pounds or thirty days!'"

It was a jolting thought. The whole time I was in panic and despair, the answer was on the way!

When our alarm clock (Bug) went away, concern about schoolchildren's getting to the bus stop on time became

Life Without Bug

a daily anxiety. Our dependence had been on his amazing built-in mechanism that could say, "OK, I'll wake you at 5:15." And he did it! Since my lowest point of activity and awareness was (and is) early morning, it was unfortunate our economy did not include a conventional waking device.

The African moon can be breathtakingly brilliant, strewing the whole landscape with liquid silver, and it was on one of these early mornings that I wakened suddenly and thought it was daylight advancing. "My watch apparently stopped at 3:00 A.M.," I thought. Knowing the children must be at the bus stop in the first pale light of the winter day, I went into frantic action. Washing unwilling faces. Dragging socks on uncooperative feet. They were like zombies, but I flew from room to room buttoning, belting, combing, and plaiting. They were eating their cereal like sleepwalkers when Dale looked at me resolutely. "Mother, I'm going to phone for the right time. It looks the same outside as when we got up." Since there was a charge for each call, this service was only utilized in emergencies. He slowly replaced the phone and faced me reproachfully. "It's only twenty minutes after four!"

They are all sending *their* children to school now, but none has forgotten how they dozed fitfully, fully dressed for school, from 4:00 A.M.—and missed the bus!

There were two reasons the children could not attend all the midweek services: the early departure for school and the fact that many of the services were held in small, overcrowded rooms, under such conditions of squalor that their presence would have been an unwise complication.

I didn't like leaving them, but Elizabeth, my dependable house help, always said, "Don't worry, Mamoruti" (a name given me by the Sesutos), "I'll keep an eye on them." Her rooms were in the outbuildings nearby, but there was the night she was called away for a family emergency after I left for church.

The service was very late, and when I turned in the driveway and saw a dining room window open, I could not get out of the car fast enough. This was trouble! I unlocked the front door to chaos. Chairs and tables were overturned, dishes and cutlery were scattered over the floor. I ran for the stairs. My children! Where were they? I passed three empty bedrooms and came to a locked door at the end of the hall. I called their names. A small voice answered, "Mommy, is that you?"

Trying to hold them all at once and to listen as they told the story of that eventful evening was a challenge. Lynda had wakened first to the growl of the dog, a peculiar squeak, and a low masculine voice swearing. The intruder downstairs tried unsuccessfully to keep a small tea table, with little, squeaky wheels, between himself and the dog. As he sparred through the living room, dining room, and kitchen with Daffy hot on his heels, Lynda roused the others.

They heard furniture falling over and dishes breaking. Then, he jumped out the window. They watched from an upstairs window as he tried to break open the door to an outside storeroom. Failing that, he attacked the garage doors. The garage was a part of the house, directly under my bedroom. They knew if he succeeded he would be back in the house. And as he was loudly declaring he would kill the dog, still harassing him, they wisely decided to lock themselves in the bedroom farthest away.

Faithful Daffy may have left some tooth marks on the frustrated burglar, but when he finally gave up and left empty-handed, she climbed in the window and waited my return at the locked bedroom door. The whole affair turned out to be a good lesson for the children in the disadvantages of disobedience. If the one who was instructed to close the back window had obeyed, the man could not have gotten in so easily (we traced his muddy tracks). And if the phone was taken upstairs and plugged in, as one had been told (a nightly ritual)—they could have called for help.

Shortly after this, Sharon developed a persistent earache that accounted for several sleepless nights. Neither prayer nor home remedies seemed to avail. Aunt Lil called her reticent Doctor Kessell, who decided an insect must have crawled into the ear. Sharon was a desperately sick little girl, not quite eight years old. The doctor feared drastic treatment could result in deafness, so lonely watches were kept, interminably it seemed, by a bed of pain.

Since our move, I had often looked longingly at the entrancing hill behind our house and wanted to climb it. One late afternoon, as I watched the shallow breath and counted the weak, fluctuating pulse beat of my child, the desire to climb that hill became intense.

"I'll go to the top and pray," I thought. "Maybe I can find healing for my daughter of the unusual, blue eyes and strength and peace for my own troubled heart."

"Sandra, dear, will you please sit by Sharon for a little while?"

Dependable, talented, patient Sandra! How often she was a bulwark of strength. I felt guilty for leaning so hard . . . so often.

I was about twenty feet from the back gate when Sandra gave a shriek that stopped me, "Mother, Mother, come quickly. I think Sharon is dying!"

I raced up the stairs and entered the room just as the abscessed ear ruptured with tremendous force, covering the pillow and a large area of the bed with foul-smelling matter, pus and the remains of a hard backed beetle that had caused all the problem. The fever was gone within an hour, and though the lovely eyes looked even bluer in a wan face, we advanced under clear skies once more, dark shadows of another valley behind us.

That hill, framed by my kitchen window, lush green in summer, tan gold in winter, has been a source of inspiration to me for many years. I look and always say, "I will lift up mine eyes unto the hills, from whence cometh my help. My help cometh from the LORD. . . ." But I still haven't climbed it!

Lynda was my dainty fairy. We should have named her April, for her climate made rapid transitions from rain to sunshine. She could not resist scissors. Besides mounds of paper dolls and doll clothes, she ventured a few times to curtains and bedspreads—with dire consequences, of course.

Life Without Bug

Almost all of the girls' clothes were remade from the used clothing parcels we received. I was amazed in later years when a lady confessed that she was jealous of my daughters' cute clothes. "You must have spent a fortune on them," she said. Well, the trimming came from one garment, and the buttons from another. The dresses were made from ripped up pieces carefully washed and ironed and sometimes reversed.

Each project was a challenge, but a new length of material made me a little nervous. Someone once sent a lovely remnant, and I spent quite some time trying to plan two dresses—one for Sandra and one for Lynda. I wanted to be sure there was enough, so I tried the patterns this way and that. Lynda settled that problem for me by cutting a doll dress and coat out of the middle of it. Sharon and Maria got the new dresses, and Lynda got something else to remember . . . for a little while, anyway!

Maria, with her beautiful, honey blonde curls, took full advantage of being the youngest. Mrs. Clark, a school teacher who taught all of them for one grade, said, "This child is very intelligent. If she can ever be persuaded to use her mind for thinking instead of scheming to evade the things she should do or concentrating on nonconformist tactics . . ."

Maria liked school for the first two days. Her strategy to avoid going after that was to lose her regulation black oxfords and white socks, part of the rigidly required school uniform. She would toss them one by one in various yards as she came home. The socks seldom came home, but invariably, a grinning, freckle-faced lad would knock on the door.

"Lady, I think your little girl threw this shoe in our yard. I don't know why. . . ." As I thanked him, I hoped the shoes would keep on coming home until she discarded this wacky idea. They were so expensive.

———————————

Once, when flying on a black, starless night across Africa, I stared out the airplane window, feeling a little of the darkness in my heart. Suddenly, on the far horizon, there was a luminous flash of lightning, etching the clouds and outlining a world of lingering blue fire. I looked long, and it came again and again, twisting ribbons of light lacing the fleecy white clouds. The vivid pattern of "God's arrows" (David named them) thrilled me with their exquisite variance and brilliance. As I watched, my shadows lifted, and a flash of understanding illuminated the puzzling maze of life before me, revealing a clear road to travel.

In the slow motion of the passing days, November came, and one afternoon in prayer I saw a signpost in front of me reading "HIGHLANDS." The only "Highlands" I could remember was Highlands North, a suburb of Johannesburg. That was strange.

A few nights later there was a dream. I was standing by a valley covered with an ugly, black cloud. Out of the cloud came a cry of "Help! Help!" The words, however, were "Highlands! Highlands!" There was an urgency that made me feel I must do something about this place. If only I could locate it! I asked everyone I met for the next few days, but no one had heard of a place with that name. I remembered a police friend, and went to see him.

"Highlands? Oh, yes, it's an illegal squatter village about twelve miles from here." He paused and looked at me sharply. "Now, don't you get any bright ideas about going out there to preach! It's not only congested and filthy, but it's dangerous. There are often three or four families to each hovel. Criminals from both Pretoria and Johannesburg hide out there, and the police only go there in armored cars, and that in the daytime. The people will all be moved away some day, and bulldozers will level the place. Eventually, it will become an elite suburb of Pretoria."

Later that day, as I turned onto a deeply rutted road, passed a protective screen of eucalyptus trees, and entered into the dilapidated squalor that was Highlands, I was confident I had come in the will of God. I shared my burden with a schoolteacher who answered in a snort of disgust: "You are crazy! No one dares go out of the house at night."

I found a level place next door to a tiny shop, and talked to the proprietor who lived in two rooms tacked on the back. He had several more degrees of courtesy but no hope of success with my project.

"Put a tent there for gospel services? Lady, it would probably be cut down and burned within twenty-four hours. This place may need your gospel—but I don't think they want it!"

I drove up and down, round and round, over precarious trails, looking, hoping. And then, beside a better section of the road (naturally, graveled), I saw the level remains of an old tennis court. Nearby, on an elevated area, was a butcher shop and the owner's house. It looked ideal. I tried a different approach this time. "Mr. Davis, I would like to erect a tent on the old tennis court for gospel services. Do you have any objections?"

He came from behind the chopping block, wiping his hands on his apron, and walked with me to the edge of the rise. "Have you considered that it might be dangerous?" I stated my case and waited.

"Well, I'm not a religious man, but I have been concerned about my children growing up without a church. There is no doubt that this community needs to learn something about God. . . ." He stared at the depressing scene for several minutes, then said decisively: "All right, Mrs. Freeman, against my better judgment, I'll be your ally. You can leave your pressure lanterns at my house, and I'll try to keep a watch on the tent when possible. Just count me out on *ecclesiastical* matters. . . ."

Between us, Dale and I remembered most of the essentials for erecting the big, three-pole tent, and it went up without difficulty. I learned later that keeping it up was a bigger problem.

We did a Pied Piper for the first service. I drove around with a trailerload of young people from the Colored Church at Claremont. Sandra played the accordion, and we all sang and invited people to the service. We started the first night with about sixty people present. The second night I came alone. Distance and expense made it impossible to take helpers every night. The car lights revealed about a hundred people waiting for me in the softly falling rain, and the tent was a confused heap on the ground.

"A twisting, sudden wind came over the hill," apologized Mr. Davis. "I ran to loosen the ropes, but the tent was down before I could get there. Sorry."

Then a confusion of other voices surrounded me from the waiting crowd.

"Will you put the tent up again?"

"Can we have church tonight?"

"Will you give up?"

"Is the tent torn up?"

"No, I will not give up. If the good Lord gives us sunshine tomorrow, I'll get the tent up again." Service tonight? I remembered the small rooms and wondered.

"Does anyone here have a room big enough that we could use for service?"

A man in the crowd answered hesitantly. "I have a room that is big enough, but, uh . . ."

"Can we use it?" I asked anxiously. Noting his reluctance, I persisted: "What's wrong with it?"

"We hold dances there on Friday and Saturday nights."

"So this is Monday night. If you'll lead the way, sir, we would appreciate that room tonight."

It was not far, and the eager crowd jostled their way in. I found myself backed up against some large clay pots. My first impulse was to hold my nose. The penetrating, offensive odor told the story of a potent home brew (often called Skokiaan) and the illegal liquor traffic transacted in this place. After prayer, I

41

taught them two gospel choruses and opened my Bible to John 7:37 and 38. The text had been impressed on my mind earlier that day, and I preached with a deep assurance of Divine guidance.

"If any man thirst, let him come unto me, and drink."

Armed with a pounding board and mallet, strong glue, canvas patches, and wire, I went out the next day and soon had the tent standing once more. It fell only three more times during the next seven weeks of services.

Interest and attendance increased every night, and soon there were thirty or forty who came forward for prayer each evening. Sandra's accordion continued to be a great help on the nights possible for her to attend. She was the only one with me during the second week, when Mr. Davis came running out of his house as my car stopped by the tent. I was surprised that he did not bring the lanterns as usual. His face was grim.

"Get in the car!" he ordered. "Drive away from here as fast as you can! There can't be a service here tonight!"

"But why? We are so near a breakthrough. I am expecting people to be filled with the Holy Ghost tonight!"

"I don't understand this Holy Ghost you preach about, but I do understand danger. A band of young hoodlums, in their late teens and early twenties, were here this afternoon and gathered rocks to stone you with." He gestured toward several piles of rocks which had not been there before. "They are hardened criminals, three of them are murderers, and they mean business. They plan to burn your tent on you after . . . ," he shuddered. "Now, will you leave?" When I hesitated, he sighed, "If only your husband were here."

Fervently, I answered, "Oh, how I wish he were!" Then, I began to consider the situation. The people who are born again in these services will have to live here. Can I teach them that the Lord will take care of them if *I* run from a threat? How can my messages be positive proof of the power of God if I act like the coward I am?

Turning to the agitated man, I said, "Mr. Davis, I am sorry to make things awkward for you, but I cannot run. Believe me, I would rather be 'rocked to sleep' than fail God. I really have no choice but to go on with this service."

"Only a fifteen-year-old girl with you," he muttered. But I could hear a small but strong whisper in my heart, "Lo, I am with you alway. . . ."

He threatened, "I won't help you pump up your lanterns." But when his sons brought them, he relented and hung the usual three outside and two inside before retreating to his front porch (with an apology) to wait for the disaster.

"Whatever happens, dear, keep smiling and keep playing," I whispered to Sandra as I began to lead our largest crowd (nearly three hundred) in song. I tried to express smiling confidence I did not feel as fleeting glances through the ragged side curtains showed ten or twelve young men outside loading their pockets with rocks. I remember sending up a silent prayer: "Lord, if You plan to deliver us, maybe You should do something soon because they look like they are about ready for action out there. . . ."

There seemed to be two leaders. Evidently, they had a difference of opinion on operational tactics, for a fierce argument developed between them. Action accelerated, and one hit the other in the nose with his fist and ran. There was a wild chase. Two laps around the tent, and then the quarry ducked inside. I did not consciously think, "This is my cue," but acted it. I was the length of the tent and shaking his hand, before anyone realized what was happening.

"Welcome to our services! I'm so glad you came." Surprise made him passive, and I led him past the rows of seats (scaffold boards laid on blocks) to the far left of the first row.

"We will teach you some nice songs about Jesus, and you will be glad you came to church tonight." I smiled at him. Though he was embarrassed by the sagging weight of his load of rocks, he stayed put. I went back to leading singing.

Outside, the gang gathered around the other leader. I did not hear them dare him to come in after his cohort but felt that was what happened. He was a big fellow, and with squared shoulders he swaggered belligerently into the tent. It could only have been the softening influence of the sweet Spirit of God that melted him as I gripped his hand in a firm shake and told him I was glad he had come. "I have a Friend who wants to meet you. He will be the best Friend you've ever had. Come with me. Let me find you a special place to sit so you can hear everything."

I led him, unresisting, to the front seat on my far right. With these two sitting at the front, I felt I could disregard the leaderless group outside. Even before the message began, they had all straggled in with their well-weighted pockets.

During the message, I kept hearing an odd noise that I could not pinpoint, a sort of soft thud. With a quick glance, I caught one in the act. Pockets were being emptied of rocks, one at a time. When the service was over, all of the rocks that had been piled outside were on the inside. Not one of them had been thrown! After service, I hired some small boys to remove them. It would be wonderful to report that the leaders were changed by God's power. That did happen to some of the gang, but the two who sat on the front seats simply disappeared. They were never seen in the neighborhood again.

The expected spiritual tide of blessings began with a likable young man a few nights later. I passed by once and noticed he was praying earnestly. Making my second pass, I observed he was sitting on the ground, looking very bewildered, holding his chin.

"Christo, why did you stop praying? Why are you holding your chin? Do you have a toothache?"

"No," he mumbled, "I don't have the toothache. I have a nervous breakdown."

"What! Have you had one before? How do you know you have a nervous breakdown?"

"When I try to pray, my chin shakes, and I can't control my tongue. It must be . . ."

"Christo, you have been asking Jesus to live in your heart, and He is moving in with the Pentecostal experience just like He gave the disciples. Don't be afraid. Let your chin shake. It's God's power, so lift your hands and praise Him!"

Never will I forget the joy and inner peace that radiated from that shy face as Christo lifted his arms in worship and began speaking fluently in a language he had never learned. He was the first of sixty-nine who received that blessing, with the same evidence, before the tent came down for the last time.

I was welcomed home one night by a group of neighbors with set faces. Among them was the building inspector and his wife, who had two sons: Nimrod, a year older than Dale, and Willie, a year younger than Dale. We called them the Three Musketeers, and many were the adventures they manufactured and shared.

A couple that went with me that night to the service left their motorcycle in the garage. I didn't think to tell Dale to leave it alone. He always (almost) obeyed me, but the problem was that I couldn't think of all the things he might do so I could say, "Don't!"

The story of the latest adventure developed as different visitors contributed disgusted bits of information. Only the parents of Willie and Nimrod were silent.

"All three of them on that motorcycle . . ."

"Whole neighborhood in an uproar . . ."

"I don't blame that desk sergeant for calling the police, his wife has been so sick . . ."

"Two of the boys had just pajamas on . . ."

"Uh, I'm sorry about all of this, folks. Where is Dale now?" I ventured timidly.

"Dale was on the back, whooping and yelling . . ." they continued.

"All the dogs in the countryside were following them and barking . . ."

I tried again, "But where is Dale?" No one seemed to hear. The disjointed accusations continued.

"Everyone out in his yard trying to find out what's going on . . ."

"Roaring up one street and down another with the police after them . . ."

"What has happened to the boys?" I asked louder, very worried by this time.

"Those wily boys! They know every shortcut through the blocks, and when it looked like the police would get there, they took off on a trail up the hill."

I had an uneasy mental picture of a motorcycle smashed on the rocks. Determined to get an answer, I stepped to the middle of the floor and demanded, "Will somebody please tell me where my son is now?"

"Oh, he's gone to bed." The motorcycle was in the garage, unharmed. I went to Dale's room. One grimy hand was clutching the sheet under his chin, and there was a large spot of grease on his pale face. I jerked the sheet off, and as I suspected, he was neither asleep nor undressed. I gave orders to get washed and ready for bed and decided the fright he received was punishment enough. Thank God—only ten days and his father would be home!

By this time, Aunt Lil, my dear friend, often spent

the night with me since the recurrence of my physical problems were unpredictable. Severe angina or a low blood pressure blackout was rather unhandy in the kitchen or halfway up the stairs.

On Thursday morning I allowed myself to start counting the days. One week! Then a cable came: "Arriving Monday." Happy shortening of days to wait. Evidently he had canceled a planned three-day layover in Rome. The proposed six-month furlough had lengthened to eight, but it would soon be over.

Aunt Lil went with me to the Friday night service in Claremont. My heart was singing over and over, "Saturday, Sunday, Monday . . . Saturday, Sunday, Monday." But on the way home, I felt a nagging uneasiness. I tried to shake it off, but the nearer we came, the more definite was the premonition of something wrong. I checked the whole house, every room, and found nothing amiss, but the feeling persisted.

"Well," said Aunt Lil, "Since you are in no hurry to go to bed, I'll bathe first." However, in seconds she came out trembling. "I can hear men talking right under the window!" I went in the bathroom and heard it, too. We had no close neighbors. The nearest house was too far away to hear a shout for help. I lifted the phone with the feeling I would find it dead. It was.

"What are we going to do?" whispered Aunt Lil.

"We are going to pray," I answered. As we knelt, I felt a calm assurance flow through me, and I remembered that angel who was promised to camp around those who fear the Lord.

"Now what?" questioned Aunt Lil after the prayer. "We have reported to a Higher Power, and He will handle it. Let's go to sleep." Usually, I need an unwinding interval, but that night I was asleep when my head touched the pillow.

When the telephone repairman confirmed my suspicion that the wire had been cut, I thought I would look for some signs of the nocturnal visitors. I forgot it in the exciting Returning Day preparations. That Monday was anything but blue when we joyously welcomed our Bug, the traveler, home.

Chapter Three

Bug Is Home

We were barely in the car leaving the airport before I queried, "Why didn't you stop in Rome? I'm glad you came early and so thankful you are here, but why? . . ."

"It was the strangest thing. I walked up to the reservation counter of BOAC (British Overseas Airway Corporation) in London and opened my mouth to say, 'Layover in Rome,' but instead, I said, 'Straight through to Jan Smuts.' While the girl wrote, I wanted to change it but couldn't open my mouth. I started back to the hotel and thought, This is not what I want; I'll go back.' I tried to turn, but my feet walked me away. So I gave up. There must be a reason."

"Must be," I agreed. "Maybe we'll know why someday."

Later that day, I was showing off the landscaping and planting we had done in Bug's absence. It was late December, early summer in South Africa. The rains had been right, and the richly blooming profusion of flowers and shrubs made our yard a thing of beauty.

Bug looked over the low, rock fence surrounding our place and saw the glint of metal in the weeds under some low, bushy trees.

"One of the children must have lost a knife out there," he said, turning to a neighbor boy following us.

"Jannie, would you bring me that knife, please?" Jannie went around to the gate obediently, and when he lifted the knife, I felt faint. It was a homemade affair, about thirty-six inches long, razor sharp on both sides, with a stiletto point and a crude leather handle.

Comprehension dawned. It lay in a spot in line with the upstairs bathroom window. We went out and took a closer look. There were clear marks where three persons had sat. They left not only the laboriously fashioned knife but some sandwiches and cigarettes as well. When that Higher Power arranged for them to leave, they were definitely in a hurry! Then I knew why I was hindered in looking for signs. My equanimity would have been in danger had I faced that fierce weapon without Bug's strong hand to hold.

On Friday of arrival week we read the disaster headlines together: "Comet disintegrates over Mediterranean." Had he gone to Rome, Bug would have been on that Thursday jet service from Europe. We paused in awed gratitude for feet that walked away.

The revival was still on in Highlands, so the official welcome service was held there. It was a triumph, with over twelve hundred people present. Bug preached a tremendous sermon, but I saw what I had not realized before. This man was sick. Later, he reluctantly admitted that he had been in constant pain for several weeks.

Regular meetings were arranged for the babes in Christ, and tent services were closed until the second week in January. This allowed us a brief respite from the rigorous schedule we had been keeping. We hoped the extra rest would relieve Bug's health problem, too.

Soon, however, the second three-and-a-half weeks of services began, and his problem was still very much with us. The worst part was not my going alone but Bug's constant pain before I left and the all-night ordeals of suffering after I returned from church. When I suggested medical advice, he answered, "Let's pray our way through this." And we tried.

We fasted and prayed, but when I found him crawling on the floor in agony, I phoned Dr. Kessell. After examination, he called a specialist, Professor Shulumburger. I will never forget that Friday when the two doctors called me in. Every word was like a physical blow.

"Your husband should have had treatment earlier. It is almost too late now." Then those most dreaded words: ". . . cancer of the anal tract." My profound shock let me hear only snatches of sentences:

". . . gangrenous tissues."

". . . polyp enlarged to four inches in length . . ."

". . . complicated surgery."

". . . impossible to remove all roots. Hope to give him two years to live."

". . . deep sedation for several days . . ."

"Bring him to the hospital at four o'clock Sunday

afternoon. The operation will be Monday morning at eight. He must not be told the seriousness of his condition. If he has any optimism, he is going to need it." Dr. Kessell had finished.

I moved automatically, doing the necessary, trying to force a cheerful face while my heart was locked in dread. Announcements were made: "Tent services to close Sunday night . . . Baptismal service at the Apies River at one o'clock Sunday afternoon."

Three families came to spend the day that Sunday. Bug lay pale and quiet.

"Daddy," I asked softly, "which one of these preachers should I ask to do the baptizing?"

He didn't open his eyes but answered, "Neither one . . . I will."

Surely he didn't understand. I tried again. "One of the preachers can officiate at the baptismal service. Which one should it be?"

"I said, 'I will'!" he said firmly.

I really didn't plan to answer as I did, but before thinking, I blurted, "You're too weak to even dress yourself! How in the world can you go in that river and baptize folks? There are a couple of fat ones, too!"

The answer came simply and directly: "This could be the last thing I ever get to do for the Lord. So you will help me dress and get down to the river, and when the time comes to go into the water, I believe the strength will be there."

We placed a chair for him near a sturdy tree, and as I watched him cling to it, I wished there was only one to baptize instead of eleven.

Bug Is Home

"Bug, are you going through with it?" I whispered. "Are you able?" He stood up and leaned on me as he walked slowly to the river's edge. Anxious eyes saw a change as he stepped into the water. He squared his shoulders and said in a loud, clear voice, "Let us pray." Without faltering, he baptized eleven people in the name of Jesus, and then the twelfth came weeping.

"Oh, please, I must obey the Lord. Baptize me, too. I want to be ready when Jesus comes!" Bug complied and then walked unassisted to the car. At home, we shared communion with our friends, and at 4:00 P.M., with a desolate heart, I left him at the hospital.

It was probably best that there was still the closing-out service at Highlands that night. After church, the DeKooker family missed the last train at Johannesburg, so I had to take them home. I fell in bed at 2:30 A.M., too weary to think, which was another mercy.

The doctors had requested that I remain at home and stay in contact by phone. I started the contact at 9:00 A.M. "Still in the operating theatre," remained the same response for the next two hours.

At eleven o'clock I realized I could wait no longer. The tent must be taken down.

"I'll come back by the hospital," I thought. Dale hitched the rattling trailer to the car, and we took off for Highlands. We asked the largest boy of a motley crowd of children who gathered to watch to hold one pole's rope. He was thirteen, the same age as Dale but much smaller. I held the middle rope and had one of the boys on each end. We cajoled, then begged, and finally commanded the kids to stay out of the way, but just when I yelled, "Let go!" a nut brown, little boy in his birthday suit ran right in the path of my falling pole.

"O God, help me!" I gasped as I grabbed the rope and swung with all my might, hoping to deflect the pole from his course. I succeeded . . . it missed him at least an inch! He went howling down the road. My hands were a mess, and I would have liked to paddle his behind, but the strongest feeling I had was relief.

I tidied myself as much as possible, parked the car and tent-loaded trailer in front of the hospital, and walked, almost fearfully, to Bug's room. He was deathly pale but managed a smile.

"Hi, hon."

"How are you?" I asked anxiously.

"Fine," he answered in an almost chipper tone.

I was trying to reconcile circumstances with the doctor's warnings. I realized that Bug was fully conscious, so I quickly hid my rope-burnt hands behind my back as I asked, "Don't you have any pain?"

"No, do you want me to have some pain?"

"Of course not, but are you sure you don't hurt . . . not even a little?"

"I guess I could arrange for some hurting if that's what you want," Bug said with a deadpan expression on his face.

I couldn't believe my ears or eyes. Baffled, I thought I'd better change the subject. I told Bug goodbye and left to go home and to store the tent in the garage. As I walked in the front door, the phone was ringing.

Bug Is Home

"Mrs. Freeman? This is Professor Shulumburger. I've been trying to reach you all morning. I have some wonderful news. Somewhere between the final examination and surgery this morning, a power higher than ours intervened. I have never seen anything like this before. That growth looked like a shriveled, end-of-season peach. It had shrunk to the size of my first thumb joint. We clipped it off and took three stitches. There were no roots. If nothing worse than this comes his way, your husband will live to be an old man!"

In a daze of thankfulness, tears flowing, I replaced the receiver. The phone rang again, immediately. It was Dr. Kessell.

"Well, your God has performed another miracle for the Freeman family. Reverend Freeman was only on the table thirty minutes." (Someone's faulty information earlier certainly had caused a lot of mental anguish!) Whispering praises to our great Physician, I replaced the receiver, and it rang again.

"This is Dr. Kessell's nurse. Since you have done practical nursing, Mrs. Freeman, Dr. Kessell says it will be in order for Reverend Freeman to come home this afternoon. When can you come after him?" I was so excited I could hardly answer. When I helped my slow-moving but almost pain-free husband home again in less than twenty-four hours, my cup of joy overflowed.

We soon discovered that months of suffering had left their mark, and recuperation had barely begun before there was another crisis. The church group with which we had vainly endeavored to effect a working agreement when we first arrived in South Africa sent a messenger insisting we come immediately to a special meeting. We refused. They had made overtures to join us long ago but had changed their minds each time. There was definitely no compatibility, and Bug was really not able. Another preacher came and demanded our attendance, so it seemed wise to go— in spite of the disability.

We were called to stand before a crowd of about three hundred, and a spokesman made a pointed speech to the effect that all bonds, ties, agreements, fellowships, and friendships were severed from that day forward with our organization, our church in general, and us in particular. How many times have I been grateful for the amazing sense of humor E. L. Freeman was endowed with—but never more than that humiliating day. His only words, as he tremblingly collapsed into the car, were dry and without the least bit of malice: "Well, that is the first time I ever got kicked out of something I never did belong to."

———————

Dale came home from school one day all excited. "Mother, we learned about compost today. May I dig a compost hole? You can save all the potato peels and carrot tops and such things for me. It will be good for the garden after a while. May I, Mom, please?"

There had been no interest (except forced) in the garden from this quarter before, and though I had strong doubts that it would be more than a passing fancy this time, I agreed. A rather insignificant hole was dug just beyond the back fence. I looked at it a time or two, and it appeared to have only a few dry leaves in it. Yet he was a constant nuisance, wanting to snatch at peels or discarded leaves for compost. I was really puzzled when I caught him going out the back door one night with a banana, two apples, a turnip, and some carrots.

"Wait a minute, young man. Those are too good for compost." He mumbled something about thinking they were withered and under my watchful eye returned that collection to the vegetable bin. But for the next few weeks, it seemed that fruits and vegetables literally evaporated out of my kitchen.

One afternoon, two ladies came to see me. Their discussion was entirely incomprehensible at first. "It's a disgrace, Mrs. Freeman, I tell you a disgrace. That big overgrown boy with his long legs almost touching the ground."

"And some of those other children are heavy, too."

"We're ready to call in the SPCA!"

"Every time you leave, a bunch of kids come here and *pay to ride*!"

Light dawned! I thanked them for coming, and assured them the matter would be dealt with at once. I waited until we were all together that night.

"Dale!"

"Yes, ma'am?"

"So you named him Compost!" He blushed, gave his shoe concentrated attention, but made no answer.

"Where did you get that donkey, Dale? And where do you keep him?"

59

Sheepishly, he answered, "I paid two and six for him (forty cents), and I staked him out down by the Apies (nearby stream)."

Of course there was an ultimatum, and after that it was surprising how long my trips to the vegetable and fruit market lasted. Neither mention nor use ever distinguished the hole behind the back fence again.

Chapter Four

Good-bye Again, Bug

Another ultimatum was laid down in the next few days. I futilely resisted. "I can't leave you, Bug. You aren't really well yet, and besides, I have the flu. Didn't you hear me coughing last night? Whoever heard of a missionary mother going on furlough and leaving her children? I can't do it."

But the powers that be had decreed, so early in April I reluctantly boarded a Pan Am flight for my furlough—alone. Elizabeth had agreed, for a small increase in wages, to assume the added duties of all the cooking, getting schoolchildren up and off, and the mending. Her responsibilities before had been washing, ironing, house cleaning, and cooking an occasional meal.

I have never seen her equal, before or since. Elizabeth was one of those divinely provided mercies. That she loved the children and was competent and trustworthy was a comfort though I would have much preferred being there doing my part.

The airport in Accra, Gold Coast, in 1954 was a

rather shaky affair, not the spacious terminal of today's Ghana. Someone inadvertently loaded the mail sacks on asmall radioless plane making a local flight. So for many uncomfortable hours, we waited for the pilot to complete his mission and to return to the terminal in Accra. There were four tropical stops altogether. I did a little melting at each, but reaching home after six years' absence was thrilling in spite of my coughing all the way.

I knew it was an awkward time to think of anyone meeting me at the airport, but it was a rather forlorn feeling being by myself in what was now a strange land. I had never been so desperately lonely in my life—every face, accent, and manner seemed strange. Five-thirty A.M. was too early to phone the pastor whose number I had, so I rode the bus to the subway terminal.

The ride was total panic. I was accustomed to driving on the other side of the road and felt every approaching vehicle would be a head-on collision. This was my first introduction to New York and Eastern U.S. ways. In South Africa there is a sort of pleasant old-world courtesy even if sometimes hypocritical. I was not prepared for my first phone call. The pastor's wife answered with a clipped, "Yes?"

"This is Sister Freeman."

"Yes?"

"Uh, I just arrived from Africa."

"Yes?" How I wished that I was on my way back. Since I didn't know what to say next, I waited.

"Where are you?"

I decided on word economy, too. "The terminal."

Good-bye Again, Bug

"Which one?"

"I don't know."

"Find out."

I looked out the door of the phone booth and saw a man cleaning the floor. "Please, where am I?" His hearty laugh was the first refreshing sound I had heard since I left home. I repeated his answer on the phone.

"Be there in an hour. Get a magazine to read."

I was engrossed in catching up on American culture when I thought I heard, "Sister Freeman!" I looked up to see the retreating back of a slender lady clicking her heels on the double. She had my suitcase in tow. I caught up with her by the time she reached her husband, waiting in the car.

Eighty-seven blocks of that nerve-wracking traffic, and we were climbing steep, narrow stairs to the pastor's residence above the church on Ninety-second Street. She waved her hand: "Kitchen, fix breakfast if you're hungry." I wasn't. After I was oriented and developed some understanding, the pastor's wife and I had a warm friendship. But on that disjointed morning, when I heard Brother White from Illinois sound a hearty "Hello!" I could have hugged him. The wonder of a familiar face!

Downtown New York City made me dizzy. I was never so bumped and jostled. The two preachers, in exasperation, said, "Here, walk between us. You don't say, 'Excuse me,' 'I'm sorry,' and 'Pardon me' in New York City!"

There were four services which seemed like four different worlds, then a long train ride to the next appointment. Lilacs and tulips were blooming by so many front porches. I watched for and thrilled to their loveliness in passing.

I had a phone number and a warning that the pastor's wife was not well. She answered in a flat monotone. I told her who and where I was. There was a long pause, then in the same toneless voice she said, "Wait by the horse. My son will come after you later." She hung up, and she didn't say how much later or which horse she was referring to.

I looked unsuccessfully for the horse, finally inquired, and was shown a statue in the park. Two hours later, her affable son deposited me at the front gate.

"Sorry I can't come in with you, but I'm late for an appointment. Just go in and make yourself at home," he said. As an afterthought, he added, "Pay no attention to anything." I was still wondering what he meant as I knocked twice. No answer. There was the sound of animated and excited conversation inside.

"They can't hear me," I thought, so I timidly opened the door and went in. There were a half dozen boys on the floor watching a western on television. The set belonged to temporary visitors (I was later informed). One of the boys belonged to the pastor, who was away. I merited only a quick glance from them, and quickly their eyes were once more glued to the set. There was not an adult in sight, so I looked for a place to sit down. The chairs and two couches were occupied with paper, books, and coats. I perched on an overstuffed arm and waited.

Good-bye Again, Bug

Several minutes later, one of the boys yelled, "Ma! That missionary lady is here." There was no answer, and no one came. Another long wait, then the lady with the monotone came to the doorway and asked, "Tomato or vegetable?"

Startled, I answered, "I beg your pardon?"

"Tomato or vegetable . . . which do you want?" I decided she must mean *soup*, so I said, "Vegetable, please."

Time seemed to drag interminably. This was my initial encounter with television, and the noise made my head hurt and my reaction was total aversion. The chair arm was very uncomfortable, and I was seriously considering a transfer of chair contents so I could have a better place to sit when my hostess reappeared.

"Come." She gestured toward the table, where a small space had been cleared for my bowl of soup. The rest of the table was piled high with neat stacks of books, papers, boxes, and garments. Along the wall, on the staircase, and as far as I could see in every direction, the scene was the same. The lady disappeared and I ate. When I took the empty bowl to the kitchen, it appeared that every carton, bottle, or can that was ever brought into that kitchen was still there. I went back to the dining room and waited until a grown daughter came home from work and guided me to my room.

Service that night was tremendous, and the rest of the family proved interesting and friendly. The pastor, a hearty and likable man, came in just before the end of the service. He must have been uncommonly patient as well. He sent someone to the delicatessen for food and said, not unkindly, "All right, Mama, get this table cleared off, quick!" Then turning to me ruefully, he said, "She was always a wonderful woman, but now she stacks junk to the ceiling every time I leave home and won't throw anything away. Sometimes I feel tempted to strike a match to the house, but the doctors say her condition is temporary."

In later years, his loyalty and patience were rewarded when the doctor was proven right.

The next stop was Toronto, Canada, and neighboring areas. The trip proved a delightful experience in which charming new friends were made and dear old friends enjoyed.

I was extraordinarily weary as I boarded the train in Toronto, bound for Montreal. The series of services just completed were not the reason, but it was the private battle I had been fighting since I left South Africa that had not allowed me one night's good rest since arriving in America. The daytime and evening hours, which were spent with church people, were all right, but when the bedroom door closed and I was alone, the torture began. If I managed to sleep at all, it was only for an hour or so from complete exhaustion.

I could see Marla falling off the school bus and under its wheels or Sharon trying to cross the busy intersection a block and a half from our home and being struck down by a speeding car. So weird were the images before me, in vain I tried to pray and shake them off. I could hear Lynda sobbing, "Oh, Mommy, I had a bad dream. Where are you?" I could see Sandra in acute distress, and my heart ached to reach her.

The letter was *real* that I received, saying that Dale had pneumonia. This added to my distress. The imaginary scenes would vary, but they all constituted real torment. They rode with me on the train. There was added anxiety about connections out of Montreal to Presque Isle, Maine, to visit my brother, Joel. I made the mistake of trusting someone who offered to make reservations for me. Another lesson learned!

I reached Montreal and rushed to the ticket window with just twenty minutes 'til closing time. One by one the windows closed in my face, each attendant refusing to answer my questions about connections out. Lights began to go off, doors were locked, and everyone was hurrying away. Maybe the station wasn't a weird, cavernous place, but to my overwrought mind it seemed so.

Two burly, rough looking men came close to me, and started a fierce argument about whose taxi I would ride in. I was too distraught even to think where I would spend the night. Then, bless the fatherly looking, older man who stepped up, dispersed the two quarrelers with a few words, and said, "Lady, you better let me take you to the Y.W.C.A. The streets of Montreal are dangerous at night."

Though the tiny room was clean, I spent another

sleepless night—but with a difference. Just before dawn, as I stood at the window looking down on deserted streets, I realized I could not go on as I was. There were no more tears. I could not even formulate a sensible prayer, but with all my heart I whispered, "O Jesus, I need you!" My Friend came. His presence was as an arm around me—a strong shoulder to lean on.

Then, gently . . .

"Were you able to stand between your children and every danger when you were with them?"

"No, Lord."

"Who took care of them then?"

"You, my Friend." Shame burned through me.

"Why do you not trust Me now?"

"Oh, I do, dear Shepherd . . . forgive my doubting. I will trust You explicitly." I felt cleansing peace melt my fears. The glow of sunrise over Montreal echoed the glow of newborn trust in my heart.

As buoyant as the big, silver bird that flew me to Boston, my spirit soared. At last, I realized that *trusting is like breathing.* I had breathed the night before, but the rhythmic motion had to continue if I lived. It was not enough that I had trusted Jesus for this crisis or that problem, but the rhythm of trust had to be continuous if my soul lived.

The bumpy, little affair that took me to Presque Isle in a storm gave me no alarm. The battle was not won for all time, but a Mount Moriah in the background would be a continual reminder.

My brother, Joel, and his wife, Lorene, prolonged my most gratifying visit by driving me to New York, where I took the train to Morgantown, West Virginia, for a conference. Services there were tremendous, and I enjoyed the ministry of God's royalty. I then went by car to Pennsylvania for two services, then to Parkersburg, West Virginia, where I made the delightful discovery that Sister Mary Cole and I were kindred spirits.

One of my furlough problems was pinpointed for me as I zigzagged across several states. Bug met the same on his furlough. It was the collision with the preconceived ideas of missions in South Africa. We have neither mission stations nor jungles. We have tried to follow the plan of the apostle Paul with an evangelistic outreach. Every time I would forget to inform a pastor otherwise, his introduction would include some of the things he thought we did—like "walking the jungle trails" or "living in a grass-thatched mud hut." I would hang my head in embarrassment.

A simple geographical survey of the African continent's terrain might help. Listed in order of size, Africa has desert (more sand than anything else!), grassland (savannah plateaus), bush (small trees, mostly thorny), and jungle (less than ten percent of the continent).

The evidence is conclusive. That small percentage of jungle has had a lot of publicity!

I have tremendous admiration and respect for valiant missionaries contending with limited and polluted water supplies, entailing boiling and filtering; isolation; inconveniences; the responsibility of teaching their own children; constant vigilance against disease and danger; besides the awesome task of communicating the Gospel in the face of culture and language barriers. I have had extensive experience only in the communication challenge. Comparatively, I hardly feel like a missionary when I confess to having safe, running water; good schools a few blocks from home; and telephone service that has progressed from inefficient to good.

I well remember the lady that came to me at the Dallas General Conference in 1947, just before we sailed for Africa. She had talked to a South African visiting the Conference and was quite upset.

"Huh!" she said in disgust. "You aren't going to be a missionary! I've been talking to this man, and he told me all about it. Why, you will have a house to live in and even beds to sleep in. I don't call that missionary work!" She flounced away before I could even think of a suitable answer.

South Africa needs the whole gospel just as the rest of the world does. She has her own unique and well-publicized problems. We have had the strong conviction that a minister of the gospel should minister the gospel and leave politics to the professional politicians. While we do not endorse all her policies, we have obeyed her laws. Separate development has been the requirement, and within this framework, ever thankful for complete religious freedom, we have ministered the gospel to whites, tribal blacks, coloreds (mulatto), and Asiatic Indians. And God, in His mercy, has given the increase.

The quickest way out of the country would have been "going native." So we have lived in a quiet, modern neighborhood and from that central point reached out in every direction, wherever an opportunity appeared. Hauling tents hundreds of miles and camping in the car does not sound glamorous, but it was truly profitable in building the Kingdom of God.

The pastor of a church in the Midwest told me by phone that the church would be unlocked in case I came early. He and his family would only arrive in time for the service. I did arrive early and was thankful for a quiet time, which allowed me to refresh my soul with the Word and prayer. The first arrival was an all-boy lad with tan freckles, strawlike hair that had been plastered down with water but was now asserting its straight-up position, and the friendliest of snaggle-tooth smiles.

"Say, you're gonna be glad you came to church tonight. We got a missionary lady coming from Afriker."

He didn't pause for a reply. "You talk about 'ventures! She's gonna tell us all about them headhunters. They cut off people's heads and shrink them to the size of an orange." His eyes sparkled as he drew a long breath and continued. "Yeah, and she'll tell us about them cannibals! Do you know what cannibals is? They eat people! Sometimes they cook 'em, and sometimes they eat 'em raw! What do you think about that?"

I thought wryly, "I'm the wrong missionary lady."

He didn't seem to notice my lack of answers and

was starting on a vivid description of "them big snakes, nearly as long as a house, that squeeze people to death," when the pastor and quite a few folks came in. Soon the service started. After my tame description of missionary work in our part of Africa, the pastor said, "Now I want Sister Freeman to stand here in front, and all of you come by and shake hands with a real live missionary."

When my adorable little friend came by, he refused to shake hands but stood with them planted on his hips and said reproachfully, "You coulda told me!" My heart smote me. I should have.

———————

By June I was in New Mexico for a glad reunion with my mother and brothers who lived nearby. Mother suggested going to the Texas and Louisiana camp meetings in her aged Plymouth if I would drive. Then, an eccentric mutual friend asked if she could go with us to Texas. I didn't mind if she was willing to stop with us at my five appointments on the way. We found Mary Cole at our first stop. She had been organizing the Ladies Auxiliary in West Texas and needed to go to Lufkin, too. So we acquired another pleasant passenger on a hilarious journey.

One comic note was provided by the friend's basket of vegetables. She explained that she could not eat all that rich food, so she was taking what she needed for the camp meeting. She and Mother sat in the back seat, and Mother patiently and periodically

Good-bye Again, Bug

exchanged places with the bulky basket to "get it out of the sun." Whenever we stopped for gas or food, the lady diligently hunted shade for her poor, wilting beets, carrots, and turnips. Air-conditioned cars were scarce in 1954.

Sister Mary and I shared pulpits across Texas. She warmly endorsed the missionary effort, and I ardently supported the work of the Ladies Auxiliary.

A day out of Lufkin, I became very concerned about a strange noise in the car. We stopped twice at garages, but nothing could be found wrong. The mechanic would test drive—no noise. We loaded up and drove on with the sound ominously squeaking away. Sister Mary went into the post office, and I had to drive around the block. Mother smiled, "No noise . . . did you notice?"

Sister Mary got in the car, and there it was again. It was then discovered that our problem had been a twisted spring in the front seat, and no one laughed more heartily over our imaginary car trouble than the sweet lady from West Virginia.

When our "vegetarian" friend was delivered to her place of abode, she ruefully conceded that the contents of her basket had expired. "I guess it was just too hot. Would you throw these vegetables away for me, Sister Freeman?" And with that, she dumped the smelly mess on the floor of the car!

Mother and I took a brief kinfolk tour through South Arkansas before the Louisiana meeting. On our way south, we went through West Monroe to see my angel of a mother-in-law. She decided to go with us. Happy day! Two of my favorite people to travel with,

73

Mother and dear Granny Freeman, as she was lovingly known to her family and friends.

Twenty miles out of Alexandria, Mother turned and looked back as she broached a subject that was a tender point with Granny. I froze to the wheel and stared straight ahead. In our early married years, Bug and I had tried to make Granny understand that she should be baptized in the name of Jesus. Our unwise pressure had not only made her balk, but she became very sensitive about the subject. Mother climaxed her short sermon with, "Granny, dear, you have had a love affair with Jesus so long. Why don't you make it legal and take His name in baptism?"

There was silence for several miles. After we reached the Louisiana campground in Tioga and were moving our suitcases into the missionary cabin, Granny said, "Nona, would you help me find Pastor Caughron?" In between the wonderful festival of greeting old acquaintances, I looked for the pastor, eventually locating him.

Granny stepped up resolutely: "Brother Caughron, I want to be baptized. Can you arrange it?" The good pastor was not the only one with smiles all over.

Such beautiful times of fellowship and blessings come to an end, and soon we were on our way west again. I planned only a few days at Indian Village with Mother, before going on to the West Coast.

"Sis, I've been planning to make a car trade and visit friends in California for quite a while," Mother said. "If I trade the old Plymouth in on a new car, we could go together—if you will drive."

"Sounds good to me. I would much rather drive

than ride the bus," I assured her.

Arrangements were speedily made. My first appointment was Thursday night in Arizona, but a hundred miles short of our destination, something went wrong with the new car. There was a tedious wait, but finally the fault was corrected.

"This car, of course, is under full guarantee," the mechanic assured us, "but you will have to pay for the repairs and then apply to the company in Gallup, New Mexico, for a refund."

This dismayed me for a moment because it took all my cash. Then I thought, "Nothing to worry about. After all, there is the service tonight, and Mother probably has some money. . . ."

I was just thankful to get away in time. In fact, we were in time for supper, and all through that welcome meal the pastor entertained us with the price of the boat he had bought last month, the cost of the organ at the church, and the bargain they had gotten on the platform carpeting.

There was a good crowd for the service. After the preliminaries, the pastor announced, "Now, Sister Freeman is entirely supported by the Missionary Board, but we will take a small offering for her anyway. Let's give her some nickels and dimes for cold drinks, folks." I have sincerely endeavored never to let finance, or the lack of it, color my sermons, so I delivered the message God gave me as enthusiastically as He enabled me. But later, I was forced to face facts!

The total of the nickels and dimes was less than seven dollars, insufficient to buy enough gas to get to California. While we were still at church, I whispered, "Mother, how much cash do you have?"

"Nothing, dear. I paid all of my accounts before we left. Why do you ask?"

"Oh, I just wondered." The words of a song came to mind: "The Lord will provide."

"Well, Lord, there it is! You will need to multiply the dimes and nickels or the gas. . . ."

"Sister Freeman!" A determined-looking young man tapped me on the shoulder. "We have a small church on the edge of town, but if you will stay over and preach for us tomorrow night, we would appreciate it."

I tried to think. "'We have to be in Los Angeles by 3:00 P.M. Saturday. Tomorrow night is Friday. If you will let us leave immediately after church, I could drive the rest of the night and make it."

"Wonderful!" he answered. "I'll get the word around." And then with a determined look, he assured me, "The offering appeal will be for more than nickels and dimes." It was! The crowd was smaller, but the service was precious, and the $28.00 they gave took us to Los Angeles and even provided a three-hour rest in a motel on the way.

I enjoyed my first trip to California with Mother as guide. There were several unique services, and I met many wonderful people. We made a wide swing through Oregon and Colorado before our ways parted at Amarillo, Texas. She drove home, and I went on my gypsy way. After several years of incompatibility, my mother and father finally separated in the second year of my marriage. I felt keenly Mother's struggles to raise her five sons alone, with no financial assistance, so I made no effort to see Dad before I left the country.

In Africa, one night in prayer, the Lord let me know that my attitude was not right toward my dad. He was still my father, and I should love him as such, no matter what had happened. On my way to see him in Plainview, Texas, I was troubled. There was genuine love in my heart for Daddy, but what about Margie, his second wife? Ever so sweetly, the Lord reminded me, "You have been in many homes where you were a stranger. How did you act?"

"I tried to be pleasant and courteous."

"That is the way to act in this home."

"But, Lord, what shall I call her?"

"You will be directed."

When the taxi stopped outside his grocery store, I kept on my sunglasses and my hat. "Will he know me?" But I was barely in the store before he swooped me up in his arms saying over and over, "my Sister Girl, my Sister Girl," an old pet name from my childhood.

A little girl came in about that time and said, "Margie wants a loaf of bread." He identified her as Margie's grandchild. Direction had been given! If her own granddaughter called her Margie, she would be Margie to me, too.

Later, after a delicious meal, I said, "Daddy, I am supposed to preach here tonight. Shall I call the pastor to come and get me?"

"No," he answered. "It's been a long time since I heard my gal preach, so I'll take you."

I turned to Margie with Calvary-inspired love, covering her hand with mine, and warmly invited her to come with us. She looked searchingly in my eyes.

"Do you really want me?"

I could answer sincerely as I returned her gaze. "I really want you." Though nothing else outstanding happened in that service, it was a milestone for me—having Daddy and Margie with me.

With pleasure, whenever possible, I retraced the path Bug had taken on his furlough earlier and gathered as treasures the comments and impressions he had made. One dear lady delighted me, describing the unusual song Bug had sung in their church in the native language.

"I never heard anything like it," she said enthusiastically. There is a little story behind this; among his many talents, the gift of song is not included as he is tone deaf. But the pastor kept insisting he sing an African song and would not take no for an answer. So, he obligingly started on a Zulu chorus, but after a few lines, memory failed. So he switched to the Sesuto language for a few more lines when again his mind went blank. So he finished up in Afrikaans. He stated emphatically, "Never again!"

There was a medley of patient, capable friends, who served me amicably as host, hostess, or guide. I believe their names are entered in God's permanent record. My profound appreciation, though never adequately expressed, is still deeply felt. Sometimes there were sour grapes, but so much was sweet and pleasant in between.

My only connection to one appointment brought me to the town at 10:00 A.M. The pastor's wife told me her husband was out of town. "Phone back later, please." On the second call, I suggested I take a taxi if she would give me the address. She didn't think her husband would like that. "Just phone back later, please." I made intermittent calls the rest of the day, in between aimless walks and trying to read in a noisy, grimy bus station.

The pastor returned home at 5:00 P.M., and after supper, came after me. As he ushered me into the evangelist's apartment, he said I would find everything I needed in the refrigerator. It was now 45 minutes until church time. I drank a glass of milk and fell across the bed. Then I realized there was something I needed more than food or rest, and I went to work on it—praying my way past a chunk of resentment! By God's grace, I got rid of it before church. That would have been a dangerous thing to keep.

I arrived at a church near St. Louis with an excruciatingly sore throat. I whispered to the pastor that it might be wise to have one of the able ministers present take my place as my voice was nearly gone and I felt feverish.

"I'll turn up the volume," he said implacably. "We have announced a missionary, and we expect to hear one. Don't shortchange us." I held the microphone at my lips and whispered into it for the next hour. I hoped some of it was intelligent.

An old friend came up at the close and scolded,

"Haven't you got sense enough to stop when you are sick?"

My planned hostess was not present, but another kind lady offered hospitality. "The only thing . . . we are remodeling our house . . . hope you can rough it," she said amiably.

The pastor answered for me: "Sure, missionaries can always rough it."

I declined food and collapsed, thankfully, into the bed temporarily set up in a barnlike room that was half dismantled. Nightmarish fever dreams alternated with cold sweats all night. In between hammering and sanding, my hostess tried to feed me the next day, but I couldn't swallow more than a drop or two of water. She said it was cold and raining outside, so the children and dogs were confined indoors.

I approached consciousness once as a toddler tried to share her sucker with me. Another time or two a dog licked my face, but the fever was so high I was out of focus most of the day. Late that afternoon, I saw Mother standing by me, but I thought it was a dream. Some time after that, I thought I heard Brother Stanley Chambers talking.

Mother was not a dream. She was passing through, taking some of her Indians to a conference, and heard I was in the vicinity. She phoned area pastors until she located me. When she saw how ill I was, she phoned Brother and Sister Chambers.

I don't remember their moving me to their home. I only know that when I awoke much later in that lovely pink and white bedroom, I thought I was in heaven. What an atmosphere of peace and love!

Good-bye Again, Bug

Mother had given Brother Chambers my itinerary out of my purse, and he had canceled my appointments until further notice, giving me a chance to recover. I will always believe this gracious couple saved my life.

I preached my way to the General Conference in Columbus, Ohio. My anticipation of the brilliant galaxy of talented singers and preachers was met to the full. I thought nothing could spoil the pleasure of that glorious time, but then I was told that I was scheduled to preach on Sunday night.

I protested with the truth; I am neither worthy nor able. And, besides, I am afraid of microphones. One makes me nervous, more than one paralyzes me . . . there were ten or twelve surrounding that pulpit! My pleading fell on deaf ears. When the time came, someone shoved me forward. I remember that I read a text, but which one was as much a blank as what I said or did. Something held me there, and I heard myself speaking. When I felt a release, I turned to get away. I was sure I had disgraced the whole missions program.

I was driving a borrowed car. As I stumbled away, I was planning to leave a note and the keys. "I'll get a taxi to the bus station and go somewhere—anywhere—to keep from facing the fine folks I have let down."

I rushed down the back steps of the platform and into the arms of Bonnie Shelton, a close friend of many years. Somehow she sensed I needed help. Then others came. That phrase, "The Lord will provide," has come true for me over and over. His timing is perfect—at the right moment His provision arrives.

Michigan, Minnesota, and Wisconsin were on my list after Conference. I was planning to leave for Africa in November. I thought about it cautiously, not daring to let my thoughts dwell long upon that beautiful word "home." Then, a letter arrived from Bug. "I hope you can raise another $1,000 and still get home in time for Christmas. We must have the money for a building project."

My appointments were far apart and poorly arranged: I doubled back and went in circles. It was nearly the end of November, and my total assets were $250. I went to a bank with the handful of small checks. I wanted to buy a cashier's check and send the money home. The clerk asked me to step into the manager's office, and she laid the checks on his desk. He said briskly, with pen raised to write, "Your name, madam?"

I suddenly became a nonentity. I didn't know who I was! In panic, I stammered, "Uh, uh, I'm sorry, but I've forgotten my name. Surely, it will come to me in a minute." He looked at me quizzically. Deeply embarrassed, I said, "I suppose you think I'm a crook, but my mind has gone blank. I can't remember my name."

He laid his pen on the desk and said kindly,

Good-bye Again, Bug

"No, a crook will give any name. Just relax, and it will come back to you."

"Oh, Freeman . . . that's it . . . I'm Nona Freeman!"

"Mrs. Freeman, you are evidently under considerable strain. Would it help to tell me about it?"

I couldn't tell the pastors where I was scheduled to preach. It would sound like *asking,* which I didn't think was right. But God bless that sympathetic, understanding bank manager! He listened carefully while I told him of our years in Africa, my husband and children there, the need, my desire to be home for Christmas, and how slowly the money was coming in.

I ended with, "My ticket to my last appointment cost $38.00 and the offering was only $41.00. That's the story of several previous weeks. Sometimes there is only $2.00 over my expenses. The $750.00 that I need seems so far away, and I'll have to leave in three weeks if I make it home for Christmas."

He wrote out the cashier's check for me and then took my hand: "Mrs. Freeman, I am not a praying man, but I am a believing one, and I believe you will be home for Christmas."

I left the bank reassured, but my ticket to the next appointment cost $39.00 and the offering, which was taken before I preached, was only $42.00. I had a talk with myself: "You are going to forget the need and concentrate on giving each service your best. The Lord can still provide in wondrous ways, and if it is His will for you not to go home for Christmas, He will give you strength to bear it."

I went to the pulpit feeling like a bird on the wing. After a particularly anointed message, the pastor called me into his office. "Sister Freeman," he said seriously, "You may have to change your sermons if you make it financially. One of my men put a check for $25.00 in your offering tonight and then asked me to tear it up. Let's see, that leaves you only $17.00. Now, do you regret preaching the way you did?"

"No!" I answered, undismayed. "I believe God gave me the message, and I preached it the way He wanted me to. Even if I had known this would happen, I would have preached the same!"

I noticed a twinkle in his eyes as he said, "Yes, he had me tear up that check and asked me to give you this one." I stared with unbelieving eyes at the figure—$500.00! I burst into tears.

"Now, look," he said, "if you feel that badly about it, I can always return it."

"No, no," I sobbed, "I don't feel badly; I feel good. This means I can go home for Christmas!"

I made reservations the next day to arrive in South Africa December twenty-first. Commitments already made hindered it from being sooner, but I was confident they would provide the other $250.00 needed— and they did.

In New York I met Brother Johnny K. Never again need any missionary arrive unwelcomed, for he was, and is, a self-appointed welcome and farewell committee of one. Many friends and Johnny saw me off, which was a long, drawn-out affair. A French plane had crashed into the pier that morning, so all international flights were delayed five hours.

After a journey that seemed unreasonably slow, I

was back in the arms of my precious family. Sandra cried all the way home. "But darling," I said, "I'm back, so please don't cry anymore."

"Mommy, it was so long," she answered. We all agreed on that, and I was thankful to be through with furloughs for awhile.

Chapter Five

Bug and Me . . . Together

"Oh, no, not again," was my first reaction to news
of the second furlough in late 1957. (The first two
were counted as one.) Bug was informed he could
bring our two oldest children as he came on furlough.
The three younger girls and I were to hold the fort
for several months—time not specified.

Sandra didn't really want to go because she was
in love with Fred Stucki, a fine young member of
our white church in Pretoria. Bug was reluctant to
leave me because my voice was completely gone,
the result of chronic sore throat for several months.
We consulted Dr. Kessell, who referred me to a specialist, whose verdict was cancer of the throat. He
reccommended treatment in the U.S.A. He forbad
me even to whisper. So my standard equipment was
notebook and pencil, and a whistle tied around my
neck.

It was a crucial time. Decisions had to be made
about a very uncertain future, and there were no
guidelines.

The findings of the specialist wrote "finished" across my ministry. Oh, how I wished I had been a better servant of the Master. Contemplating a grim future, I hit bottom one night as I realized I had already preached my last sermon. Falling into fitful sleep, I had a strange dream. I was struggling down a very dark road, falling into deep ruts, stumbling over uneven humps, and clawing my way out of pits of slush. I cried out, "Will this road never end?"

Suddenly I crested a hill, and the darkness was gone. A clear, golden light suffused a grassy plain where many people sat waiting. I walked toward them on a path paved with small white stones. A Bible was placed in my hands, and I read a text (John 21:5). "Children, have ye any meat?" A whole sermon came to me, but as I preached, the dream faded. Awake, I wondered, "Do I dare hope? Is God's mercy so great?"

Sandra decided to attend the Pentecostal Bible Institute in Tupelo, Mississippi. Sally, Fred's sister, wanted to go with her. We got permission for Dale to board at the Bible college and to go to high school. The Missions Department agreed for the three girls and I to come by boat. Bug and the three young people left by air in the middle of January 1958. Friends took the girls and me to Capetown two weeks later.

We sailed out of Table Bay about 8:00 P.M. The girls wanted to see the Cape Town lights against the backdrop of lovely Table Mountain, so we climbed to the top deck. The view was so entrancing we stayed too long. Going down the ladder, we clung precariously. The boat had plunged into the Cape rollers, aggravated by a wind storm, and we reached our cabins with great difficulty. We couldn't undress. The wind was whistling cold across the decks, and we clung to our bunks, shivering under the blankets. None of us were really seasick, but we all felt queasy.

Fortunately, by noon the next day, the rollers were left behind, and we were in a gorgeous blue and white world. Blue-green sea, azure blue sky, and dollops of white cashmere clouds reflected in tiny white crests on the waves.

The trip would have been idyllic, except I felt weaker each day. Eating became so painful I was forced to quit, and soon afterwards my throat closed completely. We were sailing in warmer seas, but I was unable to swallow even a drop of water for three days. I felt this was the end and scribbled a note for the girls to pray for me please.

Bug was at a conference in Marshall, Texas, and picked up his suitcases to walk out of the hotel room when the Lord spoke to him: "If you want to see your wife again, you must pray." He set the suitcases down, closed the door, and fell on his knees. Later, we checked the time on this, and it matched! While he interceded for me in Texas, Lynda, Sharon, and Maria knelt around my bunk and prayed.

That wonderful God of mercy touched me. I asked for a glass of water, drank all of it, and surprised myself by saying, "Thank you." This was the first time I had spoken in four months. We later learned that other friends were impressed with the thought that I was at death's door and had earnestly prayed for me about this time. I am deeply in debt on the score of gratitude to my dear Lord and His people.

The last few days of the trip were pleasant. Nineteen days at sea is a long time, and we were anxious to land. The last day out, the captain informed us we would not land at New Orleans, as originally planned, but at Mobile, Alabama. I was alarmed. Would Bug find out in time?

Being gone from America for ten years, there was much I did not remember, but I did know these two cities were far apart. We docked at noon on Sunday, anxiously scanning the small crowd gathered to meet the boat. The one we looked for was not there.

What to do? The captain's mate came by and said there was a phone in the warehouse office that we could use for local calls. While we waited our turn on the phone, someone came by and said they had piled our luggage outside as the warehouse would be closing in a few minutes. I looked in my ministerial directory and saw there was a woman preacher listed for Mobile.

Lynda tried to talk to her, but the woman couldn't understand Lynda's accent. I took the phone, praying that my voice would operate.

"Yes," she said, "I know the Freemans from Africa, but who are you?"

"Sister Freeman," I squeaked.

"This is certainly strange. Where is your husband, and why wasn't I notified that you were coming?"

I couldn't blame the dear lady for being skeptical. Lynda's "limey" accent and my distorted voice were enough to make anyone suspicious.

I tried again: "The boat came in early and changed the scheduled port of arrival. My husband was supposed to have met us, but he doesn't know where we are." More than half of that explanation was a hoarse whisper.

Lynda took the phone: "My mother has been very sick. Will you come and get us, please? There are three of us girls with her." She wanted to know where we were and asked to speak to me again. The office manager was waving his key. Everyone else was gone, and he was ready to lock up.

"All right, I would help anyone in need. Wait there . . . it may be quite awhile before we come . . . there is a hospital call to make."

The girls pulled a locker into the shade for me to sit on while they wandered around, investigating. "Mommy, there isn't a cold drink stand or phone or anything in this 'ole' place," Sharon reported. "Everything is closed."

We had been too excited to eat the noon meal on the boat and had disembarked soon afterward. Now, there was ample time to regret that lack of judgment. I wondered, too, why I had not simply called a taxi and gone to a motel. The locker was small, but I doubled my long frame on it and laid down, too weak to sit up any longer.

Nearly three hours later, the son of the pastor came. He was kind and apologized profusely. A previous appointment delayed him. It was wonderful to stretch out on a good bed at the pastor's house, but she was sure my affliction was temporary laryngitis.

"Now, you just rest awhile, and you can preach

for us tonight. My, what a surprise for my saints—a missionary!" My courage, maintained until now, plummeted. Lynda came to see about me.

"Honey, please tell the lady how long I have been sick," I whispered.

"Mother, she doesn't understand a word I say."

My hostess came back to sit by me. "Wait until Brother Vouga hears about this," she said smugly.

"Does Brother Vouga live nearby?" She told me what I should have remembered: Pritchard adjoins Mobile. I knew Bug would have contacted our good friends, the Vougas. I wanted to ask her to phone Brother Vouga as hope flared, but my throat was too painful to make another sound. I waited.

"You know, I think I'll phone Brother Vouga and tell him my good fortune. He won't believe it—a missionary landing on my doorstep!" I nodded assent brightly and held my breath as she dialed in the hallway near my door. I heard her explanation and then Brother Vouga's voice, loud with surprise: "What, Sister Freeman with you? Her husband is here. We'll be right over."

While waiting for them to come, I prayed for strength to explain the true position, and God granted it. The dear lady understood and, after she witnessed our little family reunion, let me go with good grace.

Bug had been waiting for us in New Orleans and when he learned the boat was expected at Mobile instead, phoned Brother Vouga to get in touch with the office there for the arrival time. There was a storm out in the Gulf, so Bug had waited until 4:00 A.M. and drove to Mobile in time for the Sunday morning

service. Brother Vouga quoted the office information:
"The boat will dock early Monday morning."

An appointment had been made with a specialist in
Mobile, and he summed up his examination: "I would
not call it cancer, but this is the most inflamed throat
I have ever seen. I believe three years of x-ray ther-
apy would clear it and restore your voice." He
explained in detail there would have to be six months
of intensive treatment alternated with six months of
isolated rest. For three years! The children would have
to be boarded out. The cost would be phenomenal!

Outside the office, we looked at each other. We
both knew, without words, this was not the answer.
But what now?

"Well," Bug said as he squared his shoulders,
"we'll take it day by day. For a start, I'll take you
to Tupelo to see the children."

"And then?"

"Tom Fred Tenney phoned and asked where we
planned to stay. I told him the truth . . . I didn't
know. He suggested the missionary cabin on the
Louisiana campground. There are two bedrooms but
no kitchen. We can cook at the refreshment stand. It
would be something until we could see what God is
going to do for us."

"Sounds good," I nodded, deeply touched. The
youth president of Louisiana didn't have to be concerned about missionaries at loose ends, but caring

is especially comforting when you are on the receiving end.

After a brief visit to Tupelo, we went to Tioga and settled into our temporary home. Brother Caughron, pastor from West Monroe, took us grocery shopping and paid the bill. The girls were entranced! They had never been in a supermarket before and piled the baskets high with all kinds of extravagantly priced and packaged items. When I tried to put on the brakes, I got a furtive "Shh" from our old friend.

A week after my arrival, we were with the Manguns in Alexandria, Louisiana, for the Sunday morning service. Dear, vivacious Vesta insisted I greet her ladies' Sunday school class. I said three words and whispered the rest in the microphone.

She stood with that unconquerable faith: "How many of you believe the Lord will heal Sister Freeman and she will preach for us tonight?" There were about a hundred of them, and they all believed, enthusiastically and unanimously!

"Good! Brother Mangun will announce it on the radio program this afternoon." I sputtered a little but was unable to make any real protest. I could only surrender, and I won't say without doubts. Then I remembered the sermon I preached in my dream. If I was able to preach, that would be my message.

When we sat on the platform that night, I whispered, "Bug, you better be prepared to take over. I don't know how long I'll be able to talk." My limit was still two short sentences, but when I walked to the pulpit with the open Bible in my hand, I felt as if I were centered in a shaft of light. There was the feel of the white pebbled path, and I preached for forty-five minutes without hesitation or pain. The God of miracles lives and demonstrates His power still! The touch of faith was all that was needed.

Months of suffering had left deep scars and exhaustion. Bug remembered the chiropractor he had met in Marshall, Texas, who had asked him to bring me in for treatment. We spent two weeks at his clinic. The rest and adjustments restored nerve balance and vitality. With Alexandria and Marshall behind me, I was ready for the road. Best of all, we were together! It was not planned that way, but I will be forever grateful to the all-wise Friend who arranged it.

Back in Louisiana, the Ladies Auxiliary took charge of our three youngest daughters and under the capable leadership of Vida Clark organized a never-to-be-forgotten shopping expedition in Lake Charles.

Their excitement about selecting a new dress became hysterical joy when they were convinced they could choose three a piece AND accessories AND new shoes! Brother Fuselier, intrepid gospel pioneer, planned a fishing trip for their daddy all day, and that night in the Fuselier's home, they were called on to model all their new treasures. Brother Fuselier had to blow his nose frequently and said, in his quaint French accent, "Brother Freeman, I'm afraid these girl will be too proud in all those new dress!" On his first visit to West Monroe, before I came, Bug went across the Ouachita River to visit his father in Monroe.

"Miss anything, Son?" said Grandpa Freeman, a chipper ninety-two.

"Why no, Papa. What should I miss?"

"My old, stinking pipe! I've thrown it away. You know, I've smoked, mostly pipes, for sixty-nine years. Come, walk with me down to the corner grocer." He introduced Bug to a lady working there.

"Meet my son!"

"Glad to meet you, Mr. Freeman. Which one of Grandpa's sons are you?"

Grandpa answered proudly, "This is my preacher boy. He's the one I've been telling you about. He's been in Africa for ten years."

"Praise the Lord! Brother Freeman, I'm so happy to meet you. I've heard about you ever since I was saved in Brother Caughron's church. Have you heard the glad news? Grandpa's promised to go to church one of these days!"

It was hard to believe. Bug couldn't remember his father going to church since he was a small boy.

We soon made a visit together to West Monroe. Unfortunately, Bug was scheduled at another church the night it happened. Grandpa came to church! The service was charged with the melting Spirit of God. Every time I looked at Grandpa, while I preached, he was listening Intently. During the invitation, I asked Brother Caughron, "Won't you please go ask my father-in-law to come to the altar for prayer?" He went but without success.

"Sister Freeman, you go. I think he's waiting for you." When I was a newcomer in the Freeman family and several times since, I had tried to witness to Grandpa of the born-again experience, but his answer was always obscenities. So there was a tiny spot of dread in my heart as I walked back to where he stood. In that emotion-charged moment, I was unable to plan any words of wisdom. "Grandpa, don't you think it's time you sought the Lord?"

"I don't see so good with these tears in my eyes, honey," he said. "Will you lead me up there to that altar?"

I've known moments of elation in my life but none happier than the night I led a rough, ninety-two year old sinner to the loving arms of Jesus. After all those wasted years, he became a lovable saint! How great and inexplicable is the mercy of God!

———————

Easter was a very special time. Sally, Dale, and Sandra came from Tupelo, and arrangements were made for us to camp together in a partly furnished, vacant house. We counted Sally as another daughter, and we savored every minute of that delightful weekend.

It was the year of the cancan petticoats under full skirts. The girls looked so lovely in their Easter finery, but when Bug got behind the wheel, he would groan in mock anguish: "Ruffles to the right of me, ruffles to the left of me, ruffles before and behind me!" All of us enjoyed the impromptu meals and the good-natured banter while waiting for the bathroom. A feeling persisted that it might not happen again. It didn't.

Many miles and appointments later, we were confronted with a different sort of problem: School was out, and our car was too small. The three girls fit snugly in the back seat, but where to put three teen-agers?

Sometimes the overflow came by bus. Some of the clan took welcome turns at being farmed out, and youth camps were a double blessing. Supporting the crew required us to keep moving with no slack, often splitting up. I would accept separate invitations out of necessity. It seemed we were involved in a perma-nent juggling act.

Sandra and Sally enrolled in Stamps School of Music in Dallas. We were at James Kilgore's in Houston when, with amazing understanding, he en-listed the aid of Marvin Cole in Bay City, and between them, arrangements were made for the trustworthy Chevy to be traded in on a red and white Pontiac station wagon. It was destined to be a blessing on two continents.

We went by Dallas to see Sally and Sandra, and as we lunched together, Sandra said, "Mother, I'm going back to South Africa to marry Fred, soon."

"Honey, we know you plan to marry Fred, and we agree, but don't rush. Wait until we can all go home together." We discussed the weighty subject back and forth, and she agreed to wait awhile.

We went on our busy way. Several stops later was Kilgore, Texas. Weary, after a long service, I reached to turn off the bedside light and was startled to hear the words: "None of these things move me." I didn't know what it meant and after prayer turned over to sleep.

There it was again . . . the same words! I prayed again, but no enlightenment came, and as I considered calling it a day, the same words came distinctly the third time. I reached for my Bible. "Lord, help me find that scripture."

The Bible fell open to Acts 20, Paul's farewell to the church at Ephesus. The twenty-fourth verse begins, "But none of these things move me." There was a long session on my knees with my Jesus. This was definitely a personal message to me. Remembering how disturbed and upset I could become on short notice and over small things, I realized I needed an adjustment of perspective.

It seemed I was being instructed to "hold steady" and could not help feeling it was a warning. I closed my prayer, "Lord, whatever happens tomorrow, if You will keep me, I can hold steady. By Your grace I can be unmoved."

Those who knew chose Brother Howard Goss to come tell us that Sandra was gone. She waited two weeks! Fred sent her a ticket, and she had gone back to South Africa, alone. How thankful I was for the previous night's meeting with the Lord. While I couldn't claim to being "completely unmoved," there was strength and courage that held me steady . . . even when I realized I would miss the wedding of my first-born.

It was a comfort to learn she had tried to phone but couldn't find us due to a change of appointments. Sandra hated traveling, and our uncertain way of life on furlough, with no home, was intolerable to her. She lacked only three months being twenty years old— old enough to know what she wanted.

There was a small doubt. We had just refused the

pastorate of a good church. They even offered to build us a home of our own choosing. The enemy whispered, "If there had been a home . . ." We rebuked this together with the strong determination never to consider exchanging the call of God for security. There is considerable evidence that security can be an illusion.

Soon after this, Sally decided to return home, and our children were reduced to four. Sandra had a beautiful, picture-book wedding. We were glad that her grandmother, Carrie Eastridge, could attend. This was the first of four weddings that we missed. It seemed we were always on the wrong side of the Atlantic for these momentous occasions but not by choice.

———————

Lynda spent several weeks with a friend in West Monroe. The custom was to make quick visits between appointments to the member of the family who was not traveling with us even if it meant driving many miles out of the way. On one such visit to Lynda, she gushed, "Oh, Mother, I found the most beautiful dress! It's a perfect fit . . . the most fabulous pleats I ever saw in a skirt, and the top has a big bow at the neck!"

"How much, dear, and what color is it?" She was reluctant to answer either question. She was afraid I wouldn't approve of black for a fifteen-year-old, and she knew the price was extravagant.

Bug and Me . . . Together

"Mother, please come with me! I'll try it on—you must see it on me. You need never buy me another dress if you will just get me this one. It's the loveliest ever!"

"How much? What kind of material? What color?"

"Well, it's black synthetic chiffon, permanent-press pleats, fully lined, simply gorgeous and the price . . . it was $125.00, but it's only $98.00 now. And that's a bargain!"

"Honey, listen . . . if Mommy paid that much for a dress for you, it wouldn't be fair not to do the same for the other girls. We just can't afford it. Do you understand?" Crestfallen, she nodded.

"Tell you what. Keep an eye on it, and if it isn't sold, and if the price comes down to our reach, we'll get it . . . OK?"

After that, every time we came through or called, there was a solemn report on the current price of the dress. $89.00. $79.00. $69.00. When we came to get her, it was down to $59.00. But with so many expenses, it was still out of sight. As we drove out of town, with tear-shiny eyes she asked, "Promise me, Mommy, that if you come back through here, you will go to the Palace and just see. The lady said she was sure it would come down some more." She insisted I take a look so I would know . . . in case.

I promised. A few nights later, a lady gave me $25.00 with the instructions, "Please use this for something you especially want."

I tucked it in the back of my billfold and whispered a prayer: "Lord, if You don't mind, let that dress become available for what I have."

We were not scheduled that way again, but we unexpectedly drove through. Time was pressing, and Bug had to double-park. "Please hurry!" followed me as I dashed in the Palace "to see."

When I reached the department, I thought it had been sold. It wasn't in sight. All the sales ladies were busy, so I kept looking. Then I saw a bit of pleated hem sticking out, and there it was, tucked away among the winter coats. I pulled it out eagerly and looked at the price . . . $25.00! I hurried to the counter with the money in my hand. That was the signal for all seven of the ladies working on that floor to leave their customers and surround me.

I heard one say to another in a low voice, "How did she find it? I stuck it away among the coats!"

I said the second time, "I want to buy this dress, please!"

"But, Madam," one answered, "that dress won't fit you. You must be a size sixteen, and that's only a seven."

Perplexed, I looked at their anxious faces. "I'm not buying it for myself; it's for my daughter."

Then, they all started talking at once. "Does she wear a ponytail high on her head?"

"Has she spent ten years in Africa?"

"Is her name Lynda?"

"Listen, y'all, this lady has a little of the same accent."

"Yes," I smiled, "the answer to all the questions is yes!"

Never have I seen a garment so tenderly folded and wrapped with fourteen hands fluttering over the package—and not one dry eye.

One confessed, "We hounded the manager until he marked that dress down. We hid it, waiting for her to come for it."

"Tell her 'good luck' from all of us," they chorused as I hurried away.

So the God of big miracles does little ones as well!

Far down the road, a message reached us that Grandpa Freeman wanted to see us. We squeezed out a day before we started to the West Coast. Grandpa stated his desire: "I want me and Granny to go back together." There were big tears in his eyes. "Why can't we end our days together?"

We went across the river to Granny's tiny cottage to find the answer. "I'm enjoying going to church unhindered, Son. I don't believe he has really changed."

Bug thought of business elsewhere and left with great faith. "I believe you can persuade her to change her mind, dear." This would be no small task. They had been separated for twenty-one years.

"Granny," I started, "don't you think Grandpa is different?"

"Yes, honey, when Brother Caughron baptized him, he came out of the water with such a shine on his face as I never saw. I wasn't close enough to hear if he talked in tongues, but someone said he did."

"Then, why don't you want to take him back? I

believe he has been truly converted."

Granny picked up the ever present apron and began to dab at the tears. "I'll tell you the truth, honey; I can't forgive the way he wronged me." I put my arms around her.

"Granny, dear, did you ever fail the Lord?"

"Yes, child, many times."

"Did He forgive you when you asked Him to?"

"Oh, yes, at once. I could feel it."

"Did you know that if you won't forgive Grandpa, God won't forgive you?"

I quoted from the Lord's prayer: "Forgive us our debts, as we forgive our debtors." I also quoted Matthew 6:15: "If ye forgive not men their trespasses, neither will your Father forgive your trespasses."

"Oh, pray for me," she wept.

After more tears and a sweet prayer, Granny decided it would be good for her and Grandpa to be together again. She had one stipulation: A small house must be found for them within walking distance of the church.

Bug said with confidence, "Start packing, Mama." We went to look, and there it was, just half a block from the church, a nice, little, four room house. The owner lived nearby, so in short order it was rented and arrangements were made for water, lights, and gas. We applied for a phone, and it was promised for the next day.

Grandpa was boarding, but Granny had some furniture. We found a few more needed items at a secondhand store. Most important of these was another rocking chair. The family was divided in opinion.

Bug and Me . . . Together

Some were glad for the reconciliation and helped; others were aghast and questioned, "After all these years?" But they were not divorced, only separated, and we proceeded with cleaning and polishing the little cottage.

After everything was moved in and arranged, we took them out to eat at a restaurant operated by granddaughters. Then, tired but contented, we left for Alexandria to get our children. The more I considered that day's work, the happier I was. I began to rejoice in the Lord, and His Spirit flowed over us as a river.

We praised Him in many different languages, glory-charged mile after mile. When the Spirit lifted, I asked Bug, "But how did it happen? Grandpa saved at ninety-two? A miracle, and now, this! I'll never forget the two sweet, old dears sitting in their rocking chairs, smiling shyly at each other. It is just too wonderful!"

Bug smiled and answered, "You don't remember? I do. This started two years ago when you came home from a prayer meeting in South Africa and found me with tears rolling down my face."

"Oh, yes, I thought you must have heard some bad news."

"That's what you asked. I told you I was heart-sore because that day Papa was ninety years old. I was thinking of his Godless life, and I told you I was trying to reconcile myself to the fact that my old Dad was going to hell. Then you took my hand and pulled me out of the chair and said, 'No! No! I don't care if he is ninety years old; even if he is ninety-two,

God will save him. He will!' It's a simple fact: You said it, and God did it! A word moved the mountain—the word of faith. And that's how it happened!"

———————

As we moved from church to church toward the West, one heavy thought rode with us—our just-turned-eighteen son's future. Dale lacked a few high school credits and wanted to go to college. Our budget could not accommodate this ambition, however worthy. Part-time jobs are not feasible for students in South Africa. Even before he decided to remain in the States, all of us felt the unspoken desire to make our time together as pleasant as possible. The realization was there that our days together were a fragile and fleeting treasure.

It may have been while looking out across the Painted Desert or on the rim of awe-inspiring Grand Canyon, but somewhere along there the decision was made. He would travel with us through California and the Northwest until the first of September. He would then return to Stockton to finish high school at Western Apostolic Bible College. I realized it was time for more of the stiff upper lip routine and tried not to cloud his plans with "Mother heartsore" about leaving him behind.

Here again the loving provision of a considerate Father was given. An unusual move of the Spirit so melted the congregation and pastor in a Southern California church that all were weeping with a burden for a lost world. Often, I have experienced that concern, but this night I was able to pull out the plug and ventilate my aching heart.

I had kept a tight rein on my emotions since the message came about Sandra getting married, so it was a relief to "let go." I prayed, "Lord, in the future I'll weep over Your world often, but tonight, grant me the release of tears as a mother. Help me commit my children, so loved and vulnerable, to Your keeping. Oh, help me *trust*. . . ."

The days were easier after that. In between the serious business of inspiring interest and support for missions, we built family memories by enjoying Yosemite National Park, Knott's Berry Farm, the Redwood Forest, and innumerable oddities and souvenir traps together.

In Oregon I saw something that mothers seldom see. Oh, it happens all the time, but usually not around parents. We made the home of the gracious Orion Gleason family our home for several days as we visited churches in the vicinity of Albany.

They had two daughters and a son, Turner, who was a clean-cut sixteen-year-old. One afternoon I sat in a corner writing letters. Lynda was curled up with a magazine on a couch near the front door. Turner, on the point of leaving for his part-time job, paused with his hand on the doorknob and looked at Lynda. He pushed the door partly open, looked again, hesitated a few seconds, then teased, "Say, you, aren't you going to tell me 'bye? Here I am going off to slave, and not even a good-bye!"

She lowered her magazine and answered with a long, saucy, "Goooood-bye."

Their gaze met and held. Neither looked my way. For one tender, frozen moment, they were the only two people in the world. Then, with the swish of a ponytail and a cheery wave of the hand, it was over. I've missed a lot of my children's lives, but I saw Lynda and Turner begin to fall in love.

Time came to start east again. Bug decided I should fly to British Columbia for commitments and later rejoin the family in Boise, Idaho. He and the children would drive through. As I walked into the Portland airport on my return, a merry "Hello!" stopped me.

"Gracie Yadon Weins! What a pleasant surprise!"

"Hi, Nona! I've checked your schedule, and you have an hour before the flight to Boise. Let's find a quiet place to talk. There's something I want you to tell me."

"I'm grateful for whatever brought you . . . even if it's only for an hour. I'm at your service, dear!"

As she directed me to a secluded corner, she asked, "Do you remember when we were traveling together in the interest of missions (for India) in 1944?"

"How could I forget? That was when I fell in love with the beautiful Northwest. There were not only some memorable services, but I recall our bit of mountain climbing and those protesting sore muscles. That's when I began calling you 'Groan,' and you nicknamed me 'Moan.'"

"It was fun," she answered with a reminiscent smile. "All of it . . . if you can call church services fun. But I want you to tell me about the night on the train after we left Pocatello, on our way to Denver. THAT night was so incredible. Sometimes I wonder if it really happened. I want to be sure that I have it straight in my mind, so please, tell me what happened, exactly the way you recollect it, with all the details you can recall."

It was amazing. I had often thought I would like to ask her that very question, but so many miles had always been between us, and now, she had beat me to it.

"Well," I took a deep breath, "my itinerary ended with the conference in Pocatello. You were going to Louisiana with me, and we had reservations to leave the next day. Then, about the same time, we both decided we would like to leave sooner—after the afternoon service if possible.

"We had traveled hard and were weary, and I was so lonesome for my children, who were with my mother in New Mexico. I hadn't seen them for nearly three months. Since my job was completed, I was impatient to leave. The war made changing bookings difficult, but we felt the Lord helped us—there was an upper berth available for the night.

"We boarded the train about 8:00 P.M. and greeted, in passing, a preacher's wife we knew. She was several coaches removed from us. We asked the porter to please make our bed as quickly as possible as we were desperately tired. Neither of us had a watch, so I have no idea of the time, but it must have been around 1:00 A.M. when I awoke, trembling, from a terrible dream. It was more like a nightmare.

"When you heard me sigh, you said, 'Moan, are you awake? Oh, Moan, I've just had the most horrible dream.'

"I shivered when you said that; mine was so vivid in my own mind. 'Tell me.'

" 'I seemed to be up above the train, watching the moon. It was so bright it was almost like daylight. I saw the train approach a long bridge—it looked a mile long—over a deep canyon. The walls of the canyon were almost straight down. At the bottom were jagged rocks and a deep, swift river with white sand.'

"You paused, then continued with horror in your voice that was echoed in my soul.

" 'And, Moan, just when all of the train was on the bridge, there was this violent explosion. I saw parts of the coaches, rails, and people exploding in every direction, then falling. Part of the twisted wreckage was burning and part was in the water. People were screaming and trying to crawl out of the water and the fire. Many lay dead or dying like crumpled rag dolls.'

"By the time you got that far, we were both crying, and my blood felt like ice water in my veins as I told you that I had had exactly the same dream. Identical . . . to the smallest detail! 'I believe the Lord is warning us of terrible danger. Let's pray!' We knew there were at least three of His children on the train, and He had given us the opportunity to plead for the lives of everyone else. There were perhaps over fourteen hundred souls on that train.

"We prayed, Gracie. We were so moved we didn't even bother to try to be quiet. It didn't matter if we woke up all the sleepers around us. We called aloud in anguish for God to have mercy and spare the people on that train. I've no idea how long we wept and prayed, but a sudden peace and sense of release came. We both felt it and decided the crisis was past. We could sleep again, and we did.

"There were ten or twelve of us in the lounge at the end of the car dressing the next morning when an agitated lady burst through the door. Deathly pale, she leaned against the wall.

"'Listen, all of you. I want to tell you how lucky you are to be alive this morning.' She dabbed at her eyes and went on in a calmer voice. 'I grew up next door to the conductor on this train. His daughter and I were best friends, went through school together, and were married about the same time.

"'He talked to me awhile before I went to bed last night. He woke me a few minutes ago and told me the most fantastic thing I have ever heard. He said that about two o'clock this morning he went out on the observation platform at the back of the last coach to enjoy the bright, moonlit night. He looked at his watch and was surprised to see that the train was running on time. Since the start of the war, for over three years, it has always been from twenty to forty minutes late. He couldn't understand when or where the time had been gained.

"'As the speeding wheels crossed a long bridge over a canyon, he looked down at the dark water of the river at the bottom. Then, just as the train cleared the bridge, the middle of it blew up in a fantastic blast of fire, flying rails and bridge supports in every direction. If it had not been for the time gained, most of us would be dead now.' She shuddered, and we waited. Then, with a deep breath, she went on: 'I asked him, "But why would someone try to blow up this train?"

"'"Because there are six hundred army doctors aboard, on their way to the front lines."

"'Then I asked, "But who? And how?"

"'He answered, "The *How* we will probably never know, but there is an Alien Internment Camp in that area that can possibly answer for *Who*."

"'So,' she looked at each of us carefully, 'You see why we are the luckiest people in the world!' She concluded her story with a relieved sigh.

"I came forward and said, 'May we tell you ladies something else very unusual?' And between us, we told of our dreams and the earnest prayer meeting.

"'The right word is *Blessed*, not lucky. We are not alive by chance today but by the mercy of God.'

"Do you recall how she hugged us, Gracie, and all the ladies thanked us for praying?"

"Yes, I remember, Nona, and you have recounted the whole event exactly as I remember it. Surely, we can say God is good. He *does* answer prayer."

"He is so good, and I'm so grateful He answers prayer. But one thing has worried me these fourteen years. Why didn't I get names and addresses of the lady or the conductor or even some of the other listeners? I did later cut a clipping out of a Denver paper that said the schedule we came on would be temporarily discontinued for bridge repairs, but I lost the clipping."

I made a gesture of frustration at my own stupidity.

"So, you and I are the only proof of what God did. In order for Him to get the Glory, you must write about it, Nona."

When my plane was called, we parted with a promise: "I'll try to write it, Gracie . . . someday."

A short time later, my family drove into the airport at Boise as my plane circled to land. Though the frequent separations were uncomfortable, there was the compensation of many exciting reunions.

Being together made the trip to Twin Falls a picnic. We arrived to an often repeated pattern. Brother Reynolds met us at the gate with the words, "Is there a Lynda Freeman in this car? Call operator six. There's a long distance call for you from Oregon!"

Time off for a drive through Yellowstone National Park delighted all of us. Bubbling mud, bears, and geysers set in a symphony of majestic peaks, sky blue lakes, greenery, and congeniality made for lifetime memories.

Then, it was off to Casper, Wyoming, for a brief visit with my brother.

"Mom and Dad," Dale said, "it's not long until school starts. Shouldn't I stay here with Uncle Paul and Aunt Barbara until then? You'll be going farther and farther from California . . ."

With an indefinite hope and schedule of reunion, the time had come for the separation. So we left Dale, and a part of our hearts, in Wyoming and traveled on.

Chapter Six

Down the Drain

A disturbing letter from South Africa soon caught up with us. Our youngest effort there was the White District—three churches, a few preaching places, and ten preachers.

A man we trusted wrote, "All the preachers have resigned except me. The churches have dissolved, and the native work is gone. There is nothing to come back to. You folks might as well stay in America or go to some other country. . . ."

We read the letter several times and finally lay down on the lumpy motel beds, overcome with shock and disappointment.

Big tears rolled down Bug's face. "Ten years of work gone—down the drain," he said with a deep sigh.

My thoughts flashed back to a few weeks before when we were honored by a "Freeman Night" at the high school auditorium in Rosepine, Louisiana, the community where we had pastored just before leaving on our first missionary tour. The special night had not been sponsored by the Rosepine church but by the community as a whole.

As Bug looked out over the huge crowd, many of whom we had never seen in our church, he turned to Maurice Woodhatch, a school board member and emcee for the night, and said, "Look, Maurice, don't forget . . . I'm a Pentecostal preacher!" Maurice paused for a moment, then answered, "That's what you were for the seven years you lived among us, and we'd be disappointed if you were anything else tonight."

That night was truly a time of abounding, but as I sat looking at the letter we had just received, I recognized this as a time of abasing. I was reminded of the apostle Paul who said in Philippians 4:12, "I know both how to be abased, and I know how to abound." Yes, this was a lesson that we must learn . . . a spiritual balance that must not be disturbed by either extreme.

The only sound for a long time was the roar of traffic on the highway. Then, something moved in my heart. Suddenly, despair was swept away by a wave of assurance. I don't know how it came, but I was on my feet waving the piece of paper. "This letter is a lie! I don't believe everything is gone. Maybe this man has left, but there are faithful men who are holding the truth!" The comforting sweetness of God's Spirit filled that home-for-a-night.

Bug sat up, wiping away tears. "I believe you're right. There are problems, and no doubt we have made mistakes, but by His grace we will return and build stronger and wiser." He squared his shoulders and put his arm around me as he reminded both of us, "The Book does say, 'Your labour is not in vain in the Lord.'"

We worked our way toward Indianapolis and the General Conference. On the way, there were several appointments in the St. Louis area. The schedule we received had us at different churches for Sunday night, two hours' driving time apart. Bug left Lynda and me in front of "our" church at 5:00 P.M. Alternately we sat on the steps and walked up and down the block. At 6:30 P.M. a small lady came and unlocked a side door as youngsters were gathering for "Children's Church."

She paused with extended hand. "Are you coming to our church tonight?"

"Yes."

"Where are you from?"

"Africa."

"Oh, how nice. I have friends in Africa." She hurried on down the stairs. I wondered why I didn't tell her my name.

We were still sitting on the steps when she came back. "Since you lived in Africa, maybe you could tell our children about some of the customs over there." She stressed "customs." I still didn't tell her who I was.

"Certainly," I replied, and that passed the next half hour. What irony—to discover later that the lady was Esther Wilson, a faithful, longtime correspondent whom

I had hoped to meet personally.

Lynda and I sat in the middle section of the auditorium. No one else spoke to us. Service started, and the pastor commended the young evangelist for his fine messages of the past week. He was easily identified on the platform clutching a big Bible. Lynda whispered, "Mother, I don't think the pastor knows you are supposed to be here."

"That's the way it looks, honey. There must be a mix-up in our schedule. I haven't met him before. Now I hope no one recognizes us. Let's just enjoy the service."

There were several officials present from our Headquarters staff. As the pastor welcomed each family, the evangelist became a little more fidgety. When Brother A. T. Morgan (then General Superintendent) came in with his wife, the evangelist began turning through his Bible again. I tried to shrink my long frame into the pew as Brother Morgan was called to the platform. (We pastored neighboring churches several years before we went to Africa.)

In his usual, direct manner, he said, "I went to the other side of town to hear Brother Freeman this morning, and I don't believe in being a respecter of persons, so I've come to hear Sister Freeman tonight."

The pastor went into shock: "Sister Freeman? Here? In THIS service? Not the one from Africa!" Brother Morgan obligingly pointed me out, and the pastor said, "Come to the platform, Sister Freeman, and say a few words for us." I tried to make it very few and sat down in the chair he indicated.

"That won't do," he said. "You'll have to tell us

more. Come back and tell us about the work in Africa."

"How much time should I take, Brother?"

"Take ten minutes. No, I mean fifteen minutes. No, that's not long enough; make it twenty."

I noticed the young evangelist had slumped, pale, in his chair. As I walked by Brother Morgan, he whispered, "Go ahead! Preach! Let God have His way!"

There was an evident misunderstanding, and I felt for both the young evangelist and the pastor. I was there confusing things, but all I knew to do was just whisper a prayer. "Lord, please take over for the next few minutes." And He did!

When I sat down, the pastor said, "Oh, the choir . . . I forgot the choir. Will the choir please sing." If it had been planned, the choir's song could not have been a better conclusion to the short message. While they sang, serenity covered the platform, and a spirit of conviction melted the audience as people streamed forward to pray.

All the players in this unplanned drama found it hilarious, later, at tables of fellowship. The letter informing us of the change of schedule had not reached us, and the only sad note was the other church that waited in vain for the missionary speaker that failed to appear.

The rich fellowship, worship, and expounded Word of the Indianapolis Conference were memories to store.

The warm hospitality of Bill and Daisy Stephenson became a treasure to three travel-weary girls who stayed on after Conference for several weeks.

We were in Columbus, Ohio, when our longtime friend, George Chambers, pointed out a small, neat travel trailer. "I don't suppose the Freemans could use anything like this in evangelizing in Africa, could they?"

Since I was the only Freeman present, I tried to answer calmly. He had exposed a secret hope, so it wasn't easy. "Well, uh, yes. Something like that could be very helpful in Africa."

My mind flashed back to the many weekends when we had gone out into the country for evangelism. With an interpreter in the front and a crude camping outfit in the trunk, we stopped here and there to investigate an open door and to preach. Standing in the shade of a thorny acacia tree, we would proclaim the good news to an intent audience sitting on the ground. Then, more miles to the Saturday night special that often ended at dawn.

We took turns curling up in the car for uncomfortable naps. I thought of the complete absence of privacy. Then, I thought of the many cities, towns, and villages where the faithful tent could go up for services. If only something like that little trailer was available to us.

All of this was no doubt reflected on my face, but nothing more was said until a few days later when we spoke at Brother Chambers' church on a Sunday morning. He presented our need with perception and dignity (and appropriate details) to an understanding audience.

Down the Drain

In a few minutes, pledges were taken which enabled us to be the happy owners of a gleaming, streamlined, little home that would make the gospel even more mobile when we returned to Africa. How often, in the years that followed, did we appreciate that thoughtful pastor and his willing congregation.

Chapter Seven

Headin' South... And Home

New Brunswick, Buffalo, Niagara Falls, Toronto. On and on we traveled. I flew to the Rio Grande valley to keep some commitments. Bug and the girls went back to Columbus to get a trailer hitch put on the station wagon. They pulled the trailer south through some tricky maneuvers, encountering a snow storm at Indianapolis. Meanwhile, I kept a close tab on weather reports from the balmy valley.

It was an extra grateful clan that was finally reunited in Houston. Together, we went back to our temporary home—the tiny missionary cottage on the Louisiana campground. We began to pack for our return to Africa.

There was a confusion of boxes, crates, wrapping paper, *things,* and drums jamming the small floor space. A sharp drop in temperature, cold wind, and intermittent sleet had us all hovering over two diminutive gas heaters between ventures outside. The cottage had not yet acquired a kitchen, so the stove in the trailer provided the comfort of hot coffee and chocolate.

Some surprise visitors warmed our hearts in spite of the cold weather as we were joined by my brother, Joel, and his wife, Lorene. They were accompanied by Dale, the son I had not expected to see again for at least four years. It was Christmas Eve, and we were festooning the air with our steamy breaths when Bug called everything to a halt. There was a mystery package that had accompanied us on much of our travels. I had carefully ignored secretive glances and whispers but couldn't help but know that the mystery package was my Christmas gift. Bug decided I must see its contents before it went into the drum.

My hands were so cold that help was required to open the carton. An exquisite silver tea set! I arranged it on an upended crate in the midst of unbelievable litter. Bug found the gift, worthy of a gracious home, at a bankruptcy sale. The loving secrecy that arranged this moment disturbed my composure— I hoped my tears wouldn't freeze.

We looked at each other. What a ragtag assortment of clothes we had on! Anything to keep warm. We were disheveled, weary, and extremely hungry, but somehow the splendor of the true Christmas season (unselfish love) enfolded us. Then the absurdity of the whole scene swung the emotional pendulum almost to hysteria. And with much hilarity the gleam of silver was hastily covered and consigned to the last drum.

There was a brief visit to each of several relatives in West Monroe on Christmas Day. We found ourselves as overstuffed as we had been hungry the day before.

We said good-bye for the last time to Granny and Grandpa Freeman. With a glint of tears, Grandpa put an arm around each of us. "Well, children, I won't be here when you come back again." Then, a smile came through. "But by God's grace, there is a meeting place—take a look around that Eastern Gate in God's city when you get there. . . ."

———————————

Sailing time was late December 26th, so we hurried on to New Orleans and the last service with Pastor John Thomas.

I prayed, "O Lord, this is our final good-bye to Dale. He will be on his own from here on. I would appreciate so much having something to give him as we leave."

After church, a friend came by, slipped something into my hand, and whispered, "This is for you . . . for something you may want very much." It was a tremendous feeling to be able to place a fifty dollar bill into my son's hand as we parted.

The first ten days at sea were smooth and refreshing to both body and spirit. The last nine days, however, were filled with gray skies, and we began spinning mental cartwheels, impatient with enforced idleness. There were some occasional nagging apprehensions as well. We had an estimate from the Department of Import and Excise of the South African government on the "probable" duty required to bring in our station wagon and trailer house. We had the amount they named, but there was still some uneasiness we could not shake.

Those thoughts were soon forgotten when the three girls excitedly squealed, "Mommy! Daddy! Come look! We can see land! Table Mountain is in sight!"

Substantial Mother Earth looked so good after nineteen days on the water. Sailors who had sailed much farther and harder than we ever dreamed had for decades welcomed the sight of picturesque Cape Town, nestled at the edge of Table Bay, against the stately backdrop of Table Mountain. When snowy clouds roll over the top, those who know talk of the tablecloth.

We greeted the tablecloth as an old friend. While we were waiting for our vessel, the *Ruth Lykes,* to be unloaded, we were welcomed by the Jensens, longtime friends.

Bug went down to the dock and watched as the big crane swung our possessions off—with a minimum of dents and scratches. There was a delay in waiting for the Customs Office to open the crates. There were still further delays in finding the right office, waiting for the red-tape-machine to grind its wheels, and holding his breath while the costs were calculated.

Bug's feet had lost their spring when he and Sam came home that night. "They only want four times the amount of money we have," he announced wearily. "I'll appeal this decision tomorrow."

Several days of appeals and trudging from office to office netted the same figure. There were several reasons for this. Regulations had changed since we received the estimate in answer to our query. There was a matter of so much per pound weight that no one remembered to tell us about, etc.

The Jensens' small house was overcrowded to begin with, and it seemed to get even smaller as the days went tediously by. At first, I was sure the Lord would do a miracle for us. Soon, however, I began to doubt that. Finally, I decided He didn't even know where we were and what was happening to us.

Bug kept saying, "Jesus knows. He'll provide." As every avenue of hope closed, he was still saying it, but he didn't sound too confident.

I tasted every flavor of defeat, and all of them were laced with self-pity. By the time I reached the bottom, everyone in the house was an irritation to everyone else. I gave up the whole cause as lost.

Just as I was trying to visualize our hitchhiking the thousand miles to Pretoria, Bug called. "Get everything packed. We will leave for home this afternoon!" He took great delight in not answering my "How?" or "Who?"

"Get packed!" he repeated and hung up.

We were on our way home. Du Toits Pass and the breathtaking vista of the Cape Peninsula's lush farms and vineyards were behind us. Our trusty red and white station wagon was rolling smoothly up and down the mountains with the silver caravan (as it would henceforth be known) following effortlessly.

"Tell me again . . . exactly the way it happened."

Obligingly, Bug repeated the story of the miracle. "We were walking down Adderly Street and came to Barclays' Bank.

"Sam asked, 'You do bank with Barclays, don't you?'

" 'Yes, when I have anything to bank.'

" 'Why don't you go in and ask? They might help you.'

"I didn't have much hope but went in anyway. I told the manager about our predicament and that I had banked with Barclays for ten years in Pretoria though I had been gone for a year and there was nothing in my account now.

"The man simply phoned Barclays in Pretoria and turned back to me and said, 'Keep traveling expenses, give me the rest of the money you have, and I'll give you a check for the total amount needed. This arrangement will be good for a month, and when you get to Pretoria, you can make other arrangements there.'"

"It's unbelievable!" I said.

"Honey, the lesson of trust," Bug answered, "that's what it's all about. The Lord allows these things to happen so *we can learn to trust Him.*"

Remorse swept over me as I remembered my childish despair. "I'm so ashamed of myself! I've asked the Lord to forgive my fear and unbelief . . . Oh, for grace . . ."

Bug realized what I wanted to say. A line from an old song came from our lips simultaneously, and together we said softly, "O for grace to trust Him more."